WASHINGTON SPORTS TRIVIA

Greg Oberst
and
J. Alexander Poulton

OVER
TIME
BOOKS

© 2010 by OverTime Books
First printed in 2010 10 9 8 7 6 5 4 3 2 1
Printed in Canada

The Publisher: OverTime Books is an imprint of Éditions de la Montagne Verte

Library and Archives Canada Cataloguing in Publication
Oberst, Greg, 1957–
      Washington sports trivia / Greg Oberst, J. Alexander
      Poulton.

Includes bibliographical references.
ISBN 978-1-897277-51-5

     1. Sports—Washington (State)—Miscellanea.
I. Poulton, J. Alexander (Jay Alexander), 1977– II. Title.

GV584.W27 2010   796.09797   C2009-906808-7

Project Director: J. Alexander Poulton
Editor: Carla MacKay
Cover Image: Baseball glove: © Bobbiholmes/Dreamstime.com; rock climbing gear: © iStockphoto.com/Svetlana Gryankina, skier: © iStockphoto.com/technotr; football: © Toddtaulman/ Dreamstime.com; Qwest Field, home of the Seattle Seahawks: © Patrick Hanrahan/Dreamstime.com; Safeco Field, home of the Seattle Mariners: © Frank Romeo/Dreamstime.com; golfer: © iStockphoto.com/Sergey Kashkin; speed skater: © iStockphoto. com/corepics; all other photos: © Photos.com.

We acknowledge the financial support of the Government of Canada through the Book Publishing Industry Development Program (BPIDP) for our publishing activities.

Canadian   Patrimoine
Heritage   canadien

PC: 5

Contents

Dedication

For Linda and Oliva, my girls.

Acknowledgments

I've tried to live my life with a sense of moderation, but I do allow for a few indulgences. Sports is one of them, whether it's participating in a game (usually as a fan) or just reading the sports page. The opportunity to combine one of my daily leisure rituals with my profession as a writer is one for which I'm very thankful. And for that I give a sporting fist-bump and thank you to editor Carla MacKay and the team at OverTime Books for their superb work and for the pleasure of working with them.

Introduction

Merriam-Webster defines the word "trivia" as something that is unimportant, but I think that's a good thing. In life, we need the unimportant—trivial—things to balance out the important ones. Put another way, we need a break once in a while. Sports provide that time-out. As a participant or fan, sports take us to a place where we can forget about everything else and simply have fun for a few minutes, or maybe a day—or if you're really lucky, an entire week! In that sense, sports aren't trivial at all. They're vital.

Though Washington's major pro sports teams tend to dominate the headlines and get the most ink (not that they shouldn't), you can rest assured that the state has much more for which it can both boast and hide its head. Sports can be that way—a great moment one day, a dubious moment the next and a downright wacky one after that. Washington is certainly experienced within that spectrum, and beyond. But even though we're a little short on World Series and Super Bowl championships, by the time you're finished with this book you'll be proud to have shared the state with teams like the Mariners and Seahawks, and for reasons that might surprise you. That pride will extend to the likes of William Rhodes Jr., Mira Slovak, Ray Flaherty and Frosty Westering—names that might not ring a bell like Griffey or Largent but that still belong to sports figures no less important to the fans and players who were touched by their greatness.

So relax, read on and remember it's important, but unimportant; it's sports trivia—just the way we like it.

Chapter One

America's Pastime is Washington's Favorite

Without question, the sport with the richest history in the state of Washington is baseball. Until the major-league Seattle Pilots came along in 1969, though, baseball around the state could climb no higher than the minor leagues. Still, the game was extremely popular around Washington into and throughout the 20th century, with many legendary names and landmarks taking their rightful place in state history.

The baseball story in Washington is loaded with great teams and colorful characters and is accented with a clumsy but ultimately successful leap into the big leagues—a step that flavored baseball history in these parts with some of the most fascinating, if not sometimes the most bizarre, trivia you'll ever read about.

Play ball.

In the Beginning

In July 1872, the first baseball club was formed in Seattle. The team was called the Dolly Vardens, named after the common char species of fish found in the North Pacific waters around the state of Washington. The fish got its name from a character in Charles Dickens' novel *Barnaby Rudge*.

The Father of Seattle Baseball

Daniel Dugdale, an ex-major leaguer who coached the Seattle Giants and other teams in the area in the early 1900s, is generally thought of as the father of Seattle baseball. With its double-deck grandstand, Dugdale Park opened in 1913 and was considered one of the finest baseball stadiums on the West Coast. In 1922, Dugdale Park even became the first stadium in Seattle to use lights for a nighttime baseball game.

Babe Ruth played in an All-Star exhibition game at Dugdale Park in 1924. He hit three home runs in nine at-bats. (Nine at-bats? Turns out, Ruth was both the fourth and ninth hitter in the lineup.) On that same visit to Seattle, Ruth visited a children's hospital and tossed autographed baseballs to fans from the top of the P-I building.

Unfortunately, Dugdale Park was torched by a serial arsonist and burned down in 1932. With the park gone up in flames, minor-league baseball was forced to play at the less-than-ideal Civic Field, near what is today the Seattle Center. The all-dirt playing surface was either rock-hard in the baking summer sun or a mud bath in the spring and fall rains. Regardless, future big-leaguers like Joe DiMaggio and Ted Williams played at Civic Field with their visiting exhibition teams. DiMaggio was said to have played well on these grounds; Williams, not so much. And it was at Civic Field in 1934 that Babe Ruth returned for another exhibition game—along with Lou Gehrig. This time the "Bambino" got only one hit in five at-bats.

Fred, Swede and the Fix

Before he became infamous as one of the so-called Eight Men Out of the Chicago Black Sox scandal, Fred McMullin played his way around the Puget Sound. He was a promising infielder on Dugdale's 1912 Seattle Giants minor-league team, but McMullin had trouble getting playing time and was sold to the Tacoma Tigers. It was in Tacoma where he found his way into the starting lineup and discovered his swing. By 1914, McMullin was hitting around .300 and gaining attention from major-league teams. Sold to Detroit that year for $2000, McMullin appeared in only one game for the big-league Tigers before bouncing his way over to the Chicago White Sox in 1916. By 1920, McMullin was fingered as one of eight players to have fixed the 1919 World Series. Among the alleged co-conspirators was Swede Risberg, who played for the 1913 Spokane Indians. McMullin was mysteriously dismissed from the subsequent trial. Risberg and the six other accused White Sox players were never convicted, though all were banned from baseball. Ironically, McMullin eventually established a second career in law enforcement.

His Team, His Stadium

Emil Sick bought the Seattle Indians of the Pacific Coast League (PCL) in 1937 and changed the team name to the Rainiers, after his brewery. He then built Seattle's first modern (at least, at that time it was considered modern) baseball stadium at the site where Dugdale Park once stood. Sick also gave his new stadium a familiar-sounding name: Sick's Stadium.

The new Sick's Stadium opened in 1938 and seated 15,000 fans. Price tag: by all accounts, somewhere between $350,000 and $500,000. More than just a new place for the minor-league Rainiers to play, the stadium represented a possible link to major-league baseball. Might this stadium some day be good enough for the big leagues?

Elvis Sighting

Sick's Stadium could wait for the big leagues—on September 1, 1957, Elvis Presley staged a concert at Sick's. Legend has it that among the 16,000 screaming teenagers in attendance was James Marshall Hendrix, who took copious notes. Thirteen years later on July 26, 1970, Jimi Hendrix staged his own concert at the stadium—his last appearance in Seattle before his death on September 18, 1970.

In other celebrity appearances, heavyweight fighters Floyd Patterson and Sonny Liston won boxing matches at Sick's Stadium in 1957 and 1960, respectively. And former Minnesota governor, Jesse Ventura, wrestled at Sicks' Stadium in 1976.

What's with That Apostrophe?

Emil Sick died in 1964, and thereafter various members of his family shared ownership of the stadium. So the Sick's Stadium name was altered slightly—to Sicks' Stadium—to reflect the new plural ownership.

The Man They Called Hutch

Few players in Washington sports history are more revered than Frederick Charles Hutchinson. Born in 1919 and raised in Seattle, "Hutch" played pitcher, catcher, first base and in the outfield while leading his Franklin High School team to baseball championships. After graduation in 1937, Hutchinson played a season with the Yakima Indians of the Northwest League before signing with the PCL's Seattle Rainiers in 1938. Emil Sick knew he had something special in Hutchinson, and big crowds came to see the local kid surely destined for the majors. As a right-handed pitcher, Hutch won his 19th game for the Rainiers on his 19th birthday, and he eventually pitched his way to a remarkable 25–7 record in that 1938 season—perhaps the apex of the golden era of minor-league baseball in Washington.

Sure enough, the majors came calling, and Hutchinson spent his entire big-league playing career pitching for the Detroit Tigers. As was the case for many pro athletes in the early 1940s, Hutchinson's career was put on hold during World War II. Hutch served with the U.S. Navy from 1942 to 1946.

After the war, Hutchinson had his best years as a major-league pitcher. For his career, Hutchinson went 95–71, with an ERA of 3.71. He was also a decent hitter, with a career .263 batting average, and was named to the American League All-Star team in 1951.

In 1952, Hutchinson was still an active pitcher for the Tigers when he was asked to manage the team. He accepted and led the team until 1954.

The man everyone knew as Hutch returned to Seattle twice after that to manage the Rainiers: in 1955 to a PCL championship, and again for part of the 1959 season before going back to the majors and managing the Cincinnati Reds. He also managed in St. Louis, but it was the Reds that he took to the World Series in 1961. In that series, Hutch and his players faced a remarkable New York Yankees team featuring Mickey Mantle and Roger Maris (the two of whom had been slugging it out all season in a chase to best Babe Ruth's single-season home-run record, eventually won by Maris with 61). The Yankees beat the Reds in five games. Still, Hutch was named major-league manager of the year.

In 1964, while still managing the Cincinnati Reds, Hutch was diagnosed with lung cancer. He died that same year at age 45.

A Name Synonymous with Hope

In 1965, the Hutch Award was established and is given each year to a major-league player who most exemplifies Fred Hutchinson's courage, honor and dedication. Past winners include Mickey Mantle (the first recipient of the award), Carl Yastrzemski, John Olerud, Jamie Moyer and Mike Sweeney.

Hutch also had a sibling who had made a name for himself: Dr. Bill Hutchinson, Fred's brother and founder of the Northwest Research Center in Seattle. Following his brother's death in 1964, Bill was moved to create a division of his center that focused exclusively on cancer research. In 1975, the Fred Hutchinson Cancer Research Center opened its doors in Seattle and went on to become one of the top cancer research centers in the world.

What Goes Around Comes Around

The 2000 Gatorade state player of the year was Puyallup, Washington, product Jon Lester. Drafted by the Boston Red Sox, Tacoma's Bellarmine Preparatory School star was pitching in the big leagues by 2006. That same year, Lester was diagnosed with anaplastic large-cell lymphoma. It was cancer, but more treatable than many other types of lymphomas. Returning home to Washington for treatment at the Fred Hutchinson Cancer Research Center, Lester beat his cancer. Rejoining the Red Sox for the 2007 season, Lester worked his way back into shape and by fall was pitching against Colorado in Game 4 of the World Series. In that game, Lester went five-and-two-thirds of an inning to become one of only three pitchers to start and win a World Series clincher in their first post-season start. Lester followed up that crowning achievement in the 2008 season when he tossed a no-hitter in a game against Kansas City.

In 2008, Lester was given the Hutch Award and was the first and (so far) only Hutch Award recipient to have also received treatment at the Fred Hutchinson Cancer Research Center.

Today, "Fred Hutch" (as the center is known) operates as an international star in the field of cancer research, yet most modern-day users know little about the man whose name is on the front of the building. Indeed, Hutch, the man who once captured the hopes and dreams of local and national sports fans, is today synonymous with hope and help on a worldwide level. And that's pretty darn neat.

The Seattle Pilots—Touch and Go

In 1967, Major League Baseball (MLB) hoped to beef up its presence on the West Coast and spark some rivalries with teams in the bay area and Los Angeles. (At least that's the way the league presented it. Behind closed doors, MLB was getting some pretty intense heat from northwest politicians who had some clout in Washington, DC—clout that could mean trouble for the league's sweet anti-trust exemption the owners held over the players.) "Coincidentally," the MLB did indeed grant the West an expansion team, the Seattle Pilots, and it was to be run by the city's Soriano brothers, Dewey and Max, for play at Sicks' Stadium. The Soriano brothers had considerable baseball experience. Max was an All-Century team pitcher for the University of Washington and later served as legal council for the PCL for which his brother, Dewey, was president. Dewey also led the front offices of the Seattle Rainiers and the Yakima Bears. Ownership was shared with William R. Daley, who had previously owned the Cleveland Indians. Daley, who had once considered moving his own Indians club to Seattle, had a 47 percent stake in the Pilots.

Seattle was granted one of two MLB expansion teams in 1967; Kansas City (having just had their club spirited away to Oakland by owner Charlie Finley) got the other. (Finley, by the way, had considered Seattle before deciding on Oakland as the new home for his Athletics, but after touring Sicks' Stadium he commented that the undersized and aging facility was "aptly named.") At long last, however, Seattle had an MLB team to add to its growing reputation as a "big league" city. Let the chest pounding begin.

But there was a catch. The league recognized from the outset that Sicks' Stadium wasn't an acceptable long-term home for the Pilots. With a capacity of only 15,000, the existing stadium not only had to be expanded immediately, but the team and city also had to break ground on a new domed stadium—because of all that rain, the American League (AL) said—by the end of 1970.

A Whole New Stadium for $1.21

Building the new stadium proved to be a larger challenge than city fathers had anticipated. But they had a clue. Prior to the AL's condition to build a new baseball facility, the city had tried and failed twice before to pass bond initiatives to fund a new stadium. The first attempt was in 1960, the second in 1966. Of these proposals, one of the most unique ideas came up during the planning of the 1962 World's Fair: a floating stadium ported on Elliot Bay near the Seattle Center. Though the idea enjoyed some measure of popularity, the concept eventually sank during the wait for another public vote that didn't come until 1966.

But in 1967, Seattle was granted the Pilots expansion team that was supposed to begin play in 1971 (which was later moved up to 1969, as you will see) with the stipulation that the stadium be ready to go by the end of 1970. Furthermore, the American Football League was in expansion mode and Seattle wanted to be part of those plans as well. Between the Pilots and the possibility of landing a pro football team, there was plenty of motivation to get something built. Seattle was on the cusp of major-league status; it just needed a stadium.

But not just any old stadium would do. Because of what the AL had stipulated, planners in 1968 had an ultra-modern stadium in mind, befitting Seattle's forward-thinking image established during the 1962 World's Fair: a domed stadium to fight off those bitter northwest elements year-round. Stadium supporters—as part of a city and county public-improvement campaign called Forward Thrust—brought in heavy-hitters like Mickey Mantle and Carl Yastrzemski to help promote the idea in the days leading up to the 1968 vote on the stadium. Campaign materials touted a new stadium for a cost of only $1.21 per King County taxpayer per year.

The 1968 campaign also promised that a "yes" vote would bring the likes of Bart Starr, Roman Gabriel and Daryle Lamonica (popular NFL quarterbacks of the day)—not to mention Mantle and Yastrzemski—to Seattle as early as the following spring. But wait, there was more! The stadium campaign promised that with a new domed facility, presidents of the United States could be seen in person, as well as great religious leaders of the time. (Were these dignitaries not welcomed in Seattle otherwise?)

And sold. Decision day came on February 13, 1968, and at long last, voters approved $40 million (though costs eventually reached $67 million) in stadium funding. Let the games begin.

Play Ball—at Last!

The Seattle Pilots got off to a pretty good start, winning their season opener on the road against the California Angels. The Pilots had loaded up on veterans—albeit, aging—and had a pretty good base stealer in Tommy Harper, who led the AL in steals in 1969. The team was managed by Joe Schultz, a longtime coach with St. Louis— including during their World Series runs in 1967 and 1968. The Pilots figured they had their man in Schultz and so they gave him a shot at his first manager position in "the Bigs." Schultz was a likable enough manager, but was not one remembered for his in-game savvy. What he was famous for was his locker-room declarations telling his players to "pound the Bud." That's "Bud," as in the beer. Turns out Schultz had a stake in Budweiser from his many days under the employ of the St. Louis Cardinals—a team owned by Anheuser-Busch, the makers of Budweiser beer.

Returning to Seattle just ahead of their home-opener and shortly after their away-game success in California, Schultz and the Pilots were treated like rock stars. There was a parade and a luncheon, and a key to the city was presented to Schultz. Meanwhile, at Sicks' Stadium, crews worked like mad to get more seats installed, as required by the AL. But things were woefully behind. Stadium expansion crews had worked through brutal winter weather but ultimately fell behind schedule. By the day of the home-opener, only about 6000 additional seats had been installed, leaving the stadium well below the league's initial requirement to have 28,500 seats, in total, ready to go (remember, the original Sick's seated only 15,000).

But the show must go on, as they say. The Seattle Pilots played at Sicks' Stadium for their home-opener on April 11, 1969. Never mind that some fans for that first game had to wait outside the stadium long after the first pitch while their new seats were being installed. Never mind that the toilets stopped flushing after about the seventh inning, and players had to shower at their hotel— this was major-league baseball! Yup, it was all good. The Pilots even shut out the Chicago White Sox, 7–0. Seattle beat Chicago the next night as well, 5–1. After the earlier two-game split in Anaheim against the Angels, the Pilots were 3–1 and winners, baby! Life was good for Pilots fans.

Short Honeymoon

But the winning didn't last. By the end of April the team was 7–11. As the season approached its midpoint, the losing continued, and for fans, the novelty of the Pilots was beginning to wear off. For team ownership, the inadequacy of Sicks' Stadium was taking its toll. With no TV contract, poor sponsorship support and fewer and fewer gate receipts because of dwindling crowds, the Soriano brothers were losing money hand over fist. Whispers of bankruptcy along with perceived threats to fans and sponsors to step up support or suffer the consequences only deepened the bad mojo.

The Seattle Pilots ultimately lost 98 games and won 64 to finish last in the AL West in the 1969 season. But the most disappointing number of all was probably a total home-game attendance of just 677,944—far below the one million projected. In the opening game of the Pilots' final home series against the Oakland A's, only 2937 fans showed up.

So, What About that New Stadium?

Further complicating the Pilots' first season was the thorny issue of building the new stadium. In an era of protests, the anti-stadium faction wouldn't go away, arguing that public money was not well spent on private enterprises (sound familiar?). At the same time, a loud public debate about *where* to build a new stadium was raging like wildfire. A plan endorsed by the stadium commission had the superstructure going up in the Seattle Center, an idea that was defeated by voters. After countless delays because of site and design planning, ground was finally broken for the Kingdome at a location just south of downtown Seattle near the King Street train station.

All of this came at a time of economic decline in the region, as during the late Sixties and early Seventies, Boeing laid off 60,000 workers because of lost contracts with the government (such as the contract to build the Supersonic Transport—or, SST—the airplane that eventually inspired the name of Seattle's NBA team). Compelling national news was also pushing Pilots stories out of sight and mind: the moon landing, race riots and the Vietnam War, to name a few. The engine that was driving the new stadium development sputtered along slowly, putting the baseball team and city well behind in their plan to debut a new domed stadium by December 31, 1970.

While things continued to go downhill with the stadium, the team itself had hit rock-bottom. During spring training in 1970, one last attempt was made to organize local buyers for the flailing Pilots, but the deal fell through. When the Pilots officially filed for bankruptcy protection, the American League had seen enough. A willing buyer had been waiting in the wings since the end of the 1969 season: Bud Selig, a Milwaukee car dealer (legend has it that Selig made a handshake deal for the Pilots during the 1969 World Series). A Pilots equipment truck heading to Seattle was in Utah when it was stopped and instructed to wait for breaking news before going any farther. And then, just days before the start of the 1970 regular season, the truck was instructed to head east—for $10.8 million, Selig and his ownership group were given the green light to acquire the team and move it to Milwaukee.

The announcement that the Seattle Pilots were sold and moving to Milwaukee was made on April 1, 1970—April Fools' Day. Players who had started spring training as members of the Seattle Pilots were suddenly members of the Milwaukee Brewers with only four days before the start of the regular season. Thus, the Seattle Pilots became the only team in modern MLB history to move after only one season. For a city that had tried so hard—for so long—to show its big-time metropolitan might, this was a bitter pill to swallow.

Why Am I the Bad Guy?

Bud Selig, to this day, is seen by many northwestern baseball fans as something of a thief—the man who snatched away their baseball team and moved it out of town. In truth, Seattle wasn't ready for a big-league team. But that wasn't completely Seattle's fault, either. The original 1967 expansion deal with the American League called for the Pilots to begin play by the 1971 season, not 1969. The AL moved the timetable up by two years to ease the heat they were getting from a Missouri senator who didn't want Kansas City (the other expansion city, still irked about losing the Athletics to Oakland in 1967) to be without a team for another three-and-a-half years. So the timetable was moved for both teams, presumably to keep the AL's expansion plans intact. Nobody in Seattle was complaining about the date change, but the accelerated pace at which the Pilots and the city had to operate to create infrastructure befitting an MLB team only served to destroy the project altogether.

It should also be noted that in 1968, Milwaukee lost its own team, the Braves, to Atlanta. Selig was a former minority owner of the exiting team, and to replace the Braves, Selig first tried to buy the Chicago White Sox. When that attempt failed, he set his sights on the Pilots. Today, Selig is more than just the former owner of the Seattle-Pilots-turned-Milwaukee-Brewers; he is also the commissioner of Major League Baseball. So be sure to make nice the next time you see him.

Sweet Lou, Sour Trade

In spring training of their first and only season in Seattle, general manager Marvin Milkes made what was arguably one of the worst-ever trades in baseball by acquiring outfielder Steve Whitaker and pitcher John Gelnar from the Kansas City Royals in exchange for outfielder Lou Piniella. That's right, for a brief period during spring training of 1969, Sweet Lou was a Seattle Pilot. Manager Joe Schultz gave Piniella the news that he was traded in a way no other manager could when he told the rookie, "You'll have to pound the Bud in Kansas City."

With the Royals, Piniella knocked out 68 RBIs, finished with a more-than-respectable .282 average and was named the AL rookie of the year in 1969. On a more dubious note, Piniella was the first major-league player to be thrown out of the game at first, second and third bases, plus home plate—all in the same game. But that doesn't change what went on in Seattle after his trade and why management was kicking themselves. Gelnar won a measly three games during the 1969 season, and Whitaker managed only 13 RBIs.

Hello Seattle Fans, Welcome to Brewers Baseball!

Before becoming the play-by-play voice of the Portland Trailblazers, Bill Schonely was part of the two-man announcer team—with Jimmy Dudley—for the Seattle Pilots radio broadcasts. In the documentary film *The Seattle Pilots: Short Flight into History,* Schonely recounts the strangeness of spring training in 1970 when the team changed its ownership—and name—just a few days before the start of the season. Suddenly, and quite awkwardly, Schonely and Dudley were broadcasting the play-by-plays of the Milwaukee Brewers—to a Seattle audience. But the timing of the Pilots' flight out of town couldn't have worked out better for Schonely. Later that same year, he landed a gig as the voice of Portland's new NBA team, the Trailblazers, and for the next three decades was synonymous with Blazermania.

Prior to his brief stint with the Pilots, Schonely called Western Hockey League games for the Seattle Totems from 1958 to 1969 and did radio re-creations of Seattle Rainiers baseball games. Radio re-creations were common up until the early 1970s. Play-by-play sportscasters didn't often join teams on distant away games because travel was expensive and connecting to the home station with a clear audio phone-line was dicey at best. So instead, sportscasters set up in a studio at their home radio station and re-created the game using pitch-by-pitch—in the case of baseball— information fed to them by phone or wire reports. By mixing in sound effects that included crowd noise and even the crack of a bat, many listeners never knew the sportscaster wasn't at the game.

Bouton's Ball Four

Most of the aging veterans in the Pilots' lineup played their best days in major-league baseball before joining the ill-fated expansion team in Seattle. But they did bring one thing with them that Pilots relief pitcher Jim Bouton mined and turned into pure gold: stories. Funny stories, blue stories, controversial stories and many stories Bouton's teammates felt never should have left the clubhouse. Bouton told all in his book *Ball Four*, mostly written during his time with the Pilots and then later with the Houston Astros. At the time of its 1971 release, the book stirred up controversy, not so much with fans but with the league and many of the players whose stories had been retold. In fact, fans loved *Ball Four* for its candid, behind-the-scenes look at America's favorite pastime. There was nothing else like it in contemporary literature. But in the offices of then MLB commissioner Bowie Kuhn, he and the higher-ups were having a cow over the book and asked Bouton to sign a statement that professed the book to be fiction. Bouton refused.

He was traded by Seattle to Houston late in the 1969 season and later considered himself lucky for it.

Is There Anything Still Going on With that New Domed Stadium?

It figured, of course, after the bad luck of the Pilots that the construction phase of the Kingdome wasn't meant to go smoothly. During the long-delayed and long-awaited ground-breaking ceremony on November 2, 1972, the anti-stadium faction showed up yet again and proceeded to rain on the parade. Fearing the Kingdome was going to encroach on the nearby International District, protesters chanted "Stop the stadium!" and lobbed dirtballs at dignitaries putting foot to shovel to mark the beginning the of stadium's construction. And then, beset with design problems, on-site accidents and all-around bad karma, the Kingdome took nearly four years to complete.

Sign of the Times

Despite a smattering of sentimental protests, Sicks' Stadium was torn down in 1979, and on the site now resides a nationwide-chain hardware store. Inside the store is a display of Rainiers and Pilots memorabilia, and near the front entrance rests "home plate." Aside from the memorabilia inside the hardware store, a lone sign stands as the only other reminder of the once-noble stadium. The faded wood sign can be found at the corner of Rainier Avenue South and South McClellan in south Seattle. It reads "Historic Site of Sick's

Stadium, 1938–1979, Home of the Seattle Rainiers Baseball Club."

Another Man's Gold

In the demise of Sicks' Stadium, however, one person saw opportunity. As unlikely as it sounds, legendary Washington State University (WSU) baseball coach Bobo Brayton was Johnny-on-the-spot when the landmark was torn down—he was on-hand to salvage as many of the good stadium parts as possible. What was his motivation? Money. Brayton sold off most of his stadium remnants in a fund-raiser to build his own new stadium at WSU. But he didn't sell everything, saving a few parts for installation in what is known today as Bailey-Brayton Field at WSU. Brayton won an astounding 1161 games in 33 years at WSU and is the fourth-winningest baseball coach in National Collegiate Athletic Association (NCAA) history. Among the many major-league stars who passed through his WSU program are John Olerud, Poulsbo's Aaron Sele and Yakima's Scott Hatteberg. New York Yankees great Mel Stottlemyre also played under Brayton while attending Yakima Valley College in the early 1960s.

Pilots Land in Court

At the end of the years-long debacle that included Sicks' Stadium, the Pilots and the Kingdome, it was clear that the Pilots' legacy was not to come in the form of an iconic new multi-purpose facility, no more than it was going to be found in the form of a new MLB team. Following the bitter departure of the Seattle Pilots, city and state politicians led by Washington attorney general Slade Gorton went after the American League with a breach of contract lawsuit and a demand for a new team—not to mention for the reimbursement of a few million dollars ($20 million, to be exact) for all the hassle. Finally, in 1976, after nearly seven years of legal maneuvering and litigation, the AL offered to yet another expansion team for Seattle, with the condition that the lawsuit be dropped—*and say, isn't that a nice new stadium you've got up there?*

The Seattle White Sox?

While state, county and city movers and shakers were knee-deep in court with the American League over the departure of the Seattle Pilots, another ownership group was taking shape and traveling down a different path toward bringing a major-league team back to the Northwest. The Chicago White Sox were for sale in 1975, and during winter meetings, entertainer Danny Kaye and media entrepreneur Lester Smith traveled to

Hollywood, Florida, to meet with American League owners and offer details of their bid for the White Sox. AL owners approved a deal, all right, but not the Kaye/Smith offer that would have seen the White Sox moved to Seattle. The winning bid came from former White Sox owner Bill Veeck, who now had the team for a second time and kept the franchise in Chicago. No matter. Just a few weeks later, in early 1976, the AL awarded Seattle an expansion team, again. The lawsuit was dropped, and out of the settlement came the Seattle Mariners. As for Slade Gorton, it wasn't the last time he was asked to go to bat for a Seattle sports franchise.

The Mariners Come Ashore

The Seattle Mariners played their inaugural game at home on April 6, 1977, against the California Angels. The game marked the first time two American League teams played inside a domed stadium. The opening-day pitcher for the Mariners was none other than Diego Segui, who had also pitched for the one-and-done Seattle Pilots. Thus, Segui earned the distinction of being the only major-league baseball player to have been a member of two different expansion teams in the same city. As a relief pitcher for the Pilots, Segui went 12–6, his best year in the majors. Against the Angels in the 1977 home-opener, Segui walked the first batter (Jerry Remy) and the Mariners lost, 7–0. Ironically, Segui went on to post a 0–7 record that year, his last in the majors. David Segui, Diego's son, later played for the Seattle Mariners (1998–99).

Attendance for that home-opener in 1977 was 57,762 and not quite a sellout. The Kingdome capacity for baseball games was 59,166.

Familiar Results

The Seattle Mariners went 64–98 in their inaugural season. If that win-loss record looks familiar, it should; it was the exact record logged by the Seattle Pilots in their one and only season.

For nearly the next decade and a half, the Seattle Mariners fielded abysmal teams. These teams in the early years often found themselves on the wrong side of history, such as the time Roger Clemens set a (then) single-game strikeout record, fanning 20 Mariners in Boston on April 29, 1986. The first sellout of a Mariners game at the Kingdome didn't come until 1990—the opening night of the team's 14th season. And the Mariners didn't finish above .500 until the 1991 season (83–79).

The Mendoza Line

It figures, then, that a now widely used phrase for futility was spawned from a team of which little was expected. Shortstop Mario Mendoza played for the Mariners in 1979 and 1980. He was an excellent defensive player but was a notoriously poor hitter with a batting average that floated around, and often under, .200 (though he ended up a career .215 hitter). Everybody knew about Mendoza's lack of batting skill, including George Brett, the hot-hitting Kansas City Royal. In an interview, Brett referenced Mendoza's .200 batting average as an example of poor hitting, calling it "the Mendoza Line." Other ballplayers picked up the phrase, as did ESPN's Chris Berman whose frequent on-air references to the Mendoza Line gave the term a permanent place in baseball culture.

Ironically, it was Mendoza's hot fielding during a late-season West Coast swing by the Kansas City Royals that prevented Brett from hitting .400 for the year. Brett also credited Mendoza with robbing him of numerous base hits during a series with the Mariners in 1980.

Thinking Outside the Box

After nearly four seasons as the Mariners' first manager, Darrell Johnson was replaced by former Dodgers shortstop Maury Wills late in the 1980 campaign. Naturally, the front office hoped a change in leadership would lead to a few more wins. Instead it led to a few too many confounding moments by arguably the worst manager the Mariners ever had. One of the more notable moments came in an April 25, 1981, game against the Oakland Athletics when Wills instructed the Kingdome groundskeeper to extend the batter's box some 12 inches toward the mound. With a longer box, the Mariners' Tom Paciorek, blessed with a long stride, wouldn't step outside of it and risk getting called out. Furthermore, according to Wills' logic, Mariners hitters might even have been able to cheat up in the box (move toward the pitcher) and hit Oakland's Rick Langford's curveballs before they broke. But the ploy didn't get past A's manager Billy Martin who had umpire Bill Kunkel measure the box. Busted. Wills was fined $500, suspended for two games and fired two weeks later—just a little more than a month into the 1981 regular season.

Wills was replaced by Rene Lachemann, who was also fired mid-season, two years later.

Kingdome Antics

By 1980, the novelty of the big new Kingdome stadium was beginning to wear off. Indoor baseball seemed counterintuitive to many fans who thought baseball was meant to be played outdoors. Furthermore, the drab and cavernous look and feel of the concrete stadium did little to endear it to the masses. Yes, the Mariners marketing department had their work cut out for them. Not only did they have to "sell" a losing team, but they also had to do it in an increasingly unappealing stadium.

Enter the USS *Mariner*—a ship "docked" just beyond the center-field wall. In 1987, anytime the home team hit a round-tripper, the USS *Mariner* rose up and fired off its cannons. Surely that got fans' minds off the stadium and all the losing! Then there were outfield distances measured in fathoms (as well as feet) and a couple appearances by Morganna The Kissing Bandit (first seen in the 1979 All-Star Game at the Kingdome—she ran onto the field and kissed George Brett—and then again in 1986, going after Seattle catcher Steve Yeager).

On May 8, 1982, Mariners skipper Lachemann wore a pair of funny-nose glasses to the pre-game umpires' meeting. It was all part of, you guessed it, Funny-Nose Glasses Night at the ballpark. Along with thousands of fans and owner George Argyros, Mariners relief pitchers also sported the goofy glasses as they walked across the field to the bullpen before the game. During the lineup exchange, the plate umpire said to Lachemann, "No wonder you guys are in last place."

Mariners fans did enjoy a historic baseball moment on May 6, 1982, two days prior to "Funny Nose" night, when pitcher Gaylord Perry, against the Yankees, notched his 300th career victory. Still, "Funny Nose" night outdrew Perry's attendance by nearly 10,000 fans.

From Cocktail Waiter to Hall of Fame

When the Seattle Mariners began play in 1977, they hired veteran California Angels play-by-play man Dave Niehaus to be the voice of the new franchise. And it was, of course, against Niehaus' Angels that the Mariners played their inaugural game on April 6. In the minutes leading up to the start of the game, Angels owner and Niehaus' former boss Gene Autry—the Singing Cowboy himself—came sauntering into the Mariners' broadcast booth. After an exchange of pleasantries, Autry asked Niehaus where he could get a cocktail. With the first pitch only minutes away, Niehaus stood and dashed to fetch his old boss a drink at the stadium bar near the announcers' booth. Autry didn't really thank Niehaus for his effort, but before he left the booth, the legendary actor and media mogul did mention that he felt bad for letting Niehaus slip away from the Angels organization.

Thirty-three years later, Niehaus is still the signature voice of the Seattle Mariners. And in 2008, his more than 40 years of major-league play-by-play work earned him a permanent spot in the Baseball Hall of Fame as the winner of the Ford C. Frick Award for broadcast excellence. Niehaus, also a member of the Mariners Hall of Fame, has logged some 5000 games on the air for the team and has twice been named Washington Sportscaster of the Year.

Niehaus often accented the Mariners' successes on the field with a big, "My, oh, my!"—an exclamation that is now a virtual tagline for the franchise. Other classic Niehaus-isms include his trademark home-run ("Fly, fly away!") and grand-slam ("Get out the rye bread and mustard, Grandma, it's grand salami time!") calls.

Hearing Voices

An eclectic collection of voices have teamed with Niehaus on Mariners broadcasts over the years. For instance, Emmy Award–winning sitcom writer Ken Levine worked the booth from 1992 to 1995 when he wasn't penning episodes of *Cheers* or *The Simpsons*.

Good Things Come from Finishing Last

Even though they finished with a record below .500, the 1987 Seattle Mariners were still a team worth watching. Pitcher Mark Langston set a new team record with 19 wins. Alvin Davis (aka Mr. Mariner) smacked 29 homers. Harold

Reynolds set an AL record for stolen bases. Edgar Martinez made his September major-league debut by smashing five doubles and going on a seven-game hitting streak—and hitting .372 along the way. Yes, the Mariners could be a fun team to watch—unfortunately that didn't change their usual position of dead last in their division. But by virtue of their last-place finish in 1986, the Mariners enjoyed ownership of the first pick in the 1987 draft. The team selected 17-year-old Ken Griffey Jr. It turned out to be the single most important draft pick in Seattle sports history.

Who Wouldn't Want Griffey?

And to think, the Mariners almost passed on Griffey. In the 1987 draft, owner George Argyros preferred pitcher Mike Harkey of California State University, Fullerton, over Griffey. Burned in the draft a year earlier by a high school kid, Argyros needed some deft lobbying from his executive team to be convinced Griffey wasn't also going to flame out. Argyros finally agreed, but only if Griffey was signed prior to the draft—which he was, but only the night before. Harkey, on the other hand, was taken by the Chicago Cubs and pitched eight years in the majors, going 36–36.

Early Troubled Times for Junior

As a young minor-league prospect in the Seattle Mariners farm system, Ken Griffey Jr. fell into a deep depression because of the pressure to live up to his success on the field and to the legacy of his father. In January 1988, at the age of 17, the pressure was too much for the teenager and he attempted suicide by swallowing 277 aspirin pills. "It seemed like everyone was yelling at me in baseball, then I came home and everyone was yelling at me there," Griffey recalled. "I got depressed. I got angry. I didn't want to live." Luckily Griffey was found and treated in the hospital, and today he talks to kids about his experience in the hopes of helping others avoid the same fate.

Memorable Debut

Rebounding nicely, at only 19 years old, Griffey made his major-league debut with the Mariners in 1989. As a non-roster minor-league player in spring training, Griffey wasn't expected to make the team, but he did, starting in center field. Stepping up to the plate for the first time in the regular season in Oakland, "Junior" hit a double. Then, in the home-opener against the Chicago White Sox, Griffey sent the first pitch he saw over the left-field fence for a home run. And he hit another home run the next night.

Like Father, Like Son

Considered the best professional baseball player of the 1990s, Griffey hit almost 400 home runs during his first go-around with the Mariners. One of the most memorable came after the team acquired Junior's father, Ken Griffey Sr., the first time in history a father and son played together on the same major-league team. On September 14, 1990, the 40-year-old senior Griffey hit a two-run first-inning homer off the Angels' Kirk McCaskill. Twenty-year-old Junior followed his dad with a home run of his own. The father/son duo had made history again with their back-to-back homers. In 1999, Griffey Jr. was the last player to hit a homer in the Kingdome and the last player at bat before the stadium closed. Seattle's Kingdome was the first domed stadium to be demolished. It was destroyed by implosion on March 26, 2000.

Don't Have a Cow

Ken Griffey Jr. made a memorable appearance in 1992 in the third season of *The Simpsons*, in which he was cast, along with other baseball stars playing themselves, to play on Mr. Burns' company softball team. In the episode, Griffey drinks a brain and nerve tonic that is supposed to promote robust health but in rare cases causes gigantism. Throughout the episode Griffey is seen drinking the tonic, and in the end it does cause the warned-against gigantism, and his head and feet swell to an incredible and comical size.

Griffey's ability to joke around was also evident during a 1995 spring-training batting practice when he lost a bet to manager Lou Piniella. Griffey was supposed to pay up with fresh steaks, but instead put a live, 1200-pound Hereford cow in Piniella's office.

"My People Kept Saying, 'Ken Phelps, Ken Phelps...'"

In 1988, the Mariners traded first baseman Ken Phelps for up-and-coming prospect Jay Buhner from the New York Yankees. With that acquisition, the nucleus was created for a team that took the Mariners to unprecedented success and saved Seattle from another ugly exit by a major-league baseball club. Jay "Bone" Buhner hit 307 home runs, and in his right-field, "Boneyard" became a Mariners' mainstay over 15 seasons. Further endearing to Mariners fans were Buhner's signature shaved head, jovial personality, love of baseball and appreciation of his fans—all of which were best displayed by the almost constant smile on his face.

The Buhner/Phelps trade was prosperous for the Mariners, but for legions of Yankees fans it was nothing short of a total bust. In limited at-bats, Phelps had little impact on the balance of the

Yankees' 1988 season and was traded to the Oakland A's the next year. The original trade in New York was so unpopular that it found its way into a 1996 episode of *Seinfeld*. When an actor portraying Yankees owner George Steinbrenner tells Frank and Estelle Costanza that their son George (a Yankees employee) is dead, all Frank wants to know is why Steinbrenner traded away Jay Buhner.

Mariners Fans Hadn't Heard the Last of Ken Phelps

A product of Seattle's Ingraham High School, Phelps hit perhaps his most memorable home run while playing out his career with the A's in 1990, and it came in a game against his former team. Hosting the Mariners in Oakland, Phelps was called in from the dugout to pinch-hit against pitcher Brian Holman who had retired the previous 26 batters. With two outs in the bottom of the ninth inning, Phelps hit a home run and ruined a perfect game for Holman. For Phelps, it was the final home run of his career.

Something Familiar About all of This...

Despite the perceived interest in the Mariners, by the time the early 1990s rolled around, Seattle was on the verge of losing its MLB team—again. The team was hemorrhaging dollars at the hands of an underfunded owner in Jeff Smulyan as well as dealing with stadium issues, what with the Kingdome falling apart and showing its revenue shortcomings as a multi-purpose facility.

In came our old friend Slade Gorton (by then a state senator). He was called on once more to work his magic, this time by assembling a group of local owners and one notable out-of-towner, Hiroshi Yamauchi, who was to be the largest stakeholder. The group was to be called the Baseball Club of Seattle, and, theoretically, would buy the team and keep it in town. But there was one problem: the MLB had a long-standing policy that team owners must be from either the U.S. or Canada. MLB commissioner Fay Vincent balked at the initial arrangement. However, after intense lobbying by a state congressional delegation led by Gorton, and a promise that Yamauchi would hand over controlling interest of the club to his son-in-law and Seattle-area resident Minoru Arakawa—who also happened to be the president of Redmond-based Nintendo of America—MLB owners voted to approve the sale in 1992. Unlike the Pilots the Seattle Mariners were able to turn away the moving vans and stay in the city. Yamauchi's $75-million stake in the Mariners franchise represented a watershed moment, not just in Seattle but in all of major-league baseball. For the first time in its history, MLB had a team whose majority owner was neither American nor Canadian.

Mariners a Big Hit in Japan

With the 1992 sale of the Mariners to the Baseball Club of Seattle—in which Yamauchi now held a major stake—and the subsequent signing of popular Japanese players such as Ichiro Suzuki, relief pitcher Kazuhiro Sasaki and catcher Kenji Johjima, the franchise broadened its appeal beyond the Great Northwest to become the team of the Pacific Rim. Nearly all Mariners games are broadcast live in Japan, and dozens of Japanese sports reporters routinely follow the team through the baseball season.

Sweet Lou Comes "Home"

As the Mariners slowly but surely acquired players who eventually fueled team success in the mid-1990s, there was one acquisition that put them over the top. With the naming of Lou Piniella in 1993 as the 11th manager for Seattle, the Mariners had their first high-profile clubhouse leader. He was a World Series winner as both a player (Yankees) and manager (Reds) and had "been there and done that" with some of the most famous (and infamous) players, managers and owners in all of baseball. Piniella's passion for the game was as equally impressive as his résumé.

At times, this passion got the best of him: base tossing, hat- and dirt-kicking tirades—it was enough to make even the most staid umpire quiver at the wrath of Piniella, lest they make a bad call. Twenty-four years after being traded by the Pilots to the Royals, Sweet Lou was back in town, and this time Seattle wasn't going to let him get away.

The Miracle Mariners "Refuse to Lose"

The 1995 baseball season was the year in which the Pacific Northwest experienced a quantum shift in the sport's landscape. It was a year that galvanized a relationship between fans and a team that had experienced, to that point, a luke-warm courtship at best. Long-suffering Mariners fans were enjoying a lineup teeming with tal-ent—players with redeeming personalities whom fans more than appreciated and flat-out loved. And in the Mariners manager, Sweet Lou, the fans found a man whose passion reignited their own fervor for Seattle baseball. The 1995 Seattle Mariners won baseball games—lots of them. And as the Mariners hit the mid-season, fans started to envisage the possibility of post-season play. Imag-ine that! But hopes were dashed (or were they?) as the team started a mid-season slide in August that put them 13 games behind the first-place Angels. But the refuse-to-lose Mariners surged and by mid-September had cut the Angels' lead in half. Even so, completely overtaking the Angels seemed impossible. But California continued to struggle in the last few weeks of the season while the Mariners got even hotter. "Refuse to lose" became the mantra of the late season as hero after hero stepped up for the Mariners—Randy Johnson, Edgar Martinez, Tino Martinez, Ken Griffey Jr.—and the team pulled into a tie with the Angels at the end of the regular season, forcing a one-game playoff to determine the division winner.

Meanwhile, Off the Field...

Amid some of the most exciting professional baseball the region had ever seen, developments off the field were casting a dark cloud over the whole party. Since 1993, the rain-soaked Kingdome roof had been springing leaks and was in need of constant repair. Nevertheless, the structure was deemed safe and secure. Then, just hours before a scheduled Mariners game in 1994, a 26-pound waterlogged tile collapsed onto the empty field. If the tile had collapsed just a few hours later, the results could have been disastrous.

Mariners third baseman Mike Blowers was stretching in the outfield before the game when he heard a tile hit the seats.

"We just heard a big crash and somebody said something about one of the tiles falling," Blowers recalled. *"We sat out there for what seemed like a couple of minutes until someone had the bright idea that—you know what?—those things are pretty big and maybe we should get inside (the clubhouse)."*

The Mariners were forced to play the remainder of the 1994 strike-shortened season on the road while the NFL's Seattle Seahawks moved to nearby Husky Stadium to finish out their schedule. But things went from bad to worse once crews were brought in to repair the roof of the Kingdome. During the reconstruction, two workers were killed in a crane accident.

"There were a lot of people at the time who thought baseball couldn't make it here, and they were saying, 'See, this is another example of how bad baseball is in Seattle,'" said Mariners president Chuck Armstrong. It was Armstrong, on behalf of the team's owners, who officially demanded a new stadium, or else—as the threat went—the city might lose the Mariners franchise by a move out of town or through a sale that could have the same result.

After being in use for barely more than two decades, the Kingdome was a worn out and antiquated multi-purpose facility. The new stadium, Mariners owners demanded, should be a ballpark the team could call their own. No more sharing of toys.

Flash back to the 1995 season. A red-hot Seattle baseball team was playing lights-out baseball in the late season while a ballot measure for the funding of a new stadium was being put to voters. Fan interest was high, and the crowds grew with each game because of the miracle run by the Mariners, but the stadium measure, ironically, appeared to be going down to defeat. The idea of a new stadium wasn't the issue with voters—they wanted to know how much it was going to cost and who was going to pay for it. The resulting defeat at the ballot box fueled increasing and genuine concern that the Seattle Mariners were close to becoming the Tampa/St. Petersburg Mariners, with Florida movers and shakers chomping at the bit and ready to roll out the red carpet for any team looking for a home. After all that trouble to build a new stadium 20-some years earlier, was the city, county and state possibly going to trip over itself again and lose yet another major-league team?

No, they were not going to let history repeat itself. In a special meeting, politicians in Olympia found the funding necessary to build a new stadium despite the defeat of the ballot measure. And with the team riding an unprecedented wave of success on the field, it was an easy sell to the constituency. The 1995 team had saved baseball in Seattle.

The team wasn't finished with their magic. In some ways, they were just getting started. Thanks to a coin toss, the Mariners played at home in the 1995 division decider, and Seattle beat California 9–1 behind the strong pitching of Randy Johnson and a seventh-inning bases-loaded triple by Mariners infielder Luis Sojo.

Break out the champagne. The Mariners had just accomplished one of the most dramatic pennant-race comebacks in major-league history, and because of their efforts advanced to the post-season playoffs for the first time in franchise history. This was the good news. The bad news? In their first-ever American League Division Series (ALDS), the Mariners had to face the always-tough, playoff-tested New York Yankees.

Bring on the Big Apple

The day after their big win, the Seattle Mariners flew to New York. Tired and playing on scant rest, the Mariners nearly beat the Yankees in Game 1 of the ALDS on two homers by Griffey Jr.—his second round-tripper tying the score at 4–4 in the seventh. But the wheels came off in the bottom of the inning and Seattle lost 9–6.

Game 2 was an epic, five-hour baseball game for the ages. With a 12th-inning homer by Griffey, it looked like the Mariners couldn't lose. But the Yankees tied it up in the bottom of the inning with a run-scoring double by Ruben Sierra. Then, in the bottom of the 15th, Jim Leyritz belted a two-run homer that gave his Yankees a daunting two-game lead in the best-of-five series.

The Mariners, however, had their ace rested and ready for Game 3, which was back in Seattle. Randy Johnson proceeded to toss a gem and the Mariners won 7–4. With renewed confidence, Seattle went into Game 4 believing they could take down their storied opponents. But the Yankees had other ideas, torching Mariners pitcher Chris Bosio for five runs through only three innings. Things looked bleak until Edgar Martinez stepped up to the plate in the bottom of the third. His three-run homer ignited the crowd and, ultimately, ended a four-run inning for the Mariners. Tied at 6–6 in the bottom of the eighth, Martinez got up to the plate with the bases loaded and sent a John Wetteland fastball over the fence for a grand slam (or, as broadcaster Dave Niehaus would say, "Get out the rye bread and mustard, Grandma..."), giving the Mariners a big lead, and for Martinez, a post-season record for RBIs (7). Before the inning was finished, Jay Buhner added an insurance homer. When all was said and done, Seattle had weathered a rally attempt by the Yankees and won Game 4, 11–8. Down in the series 0–2, the Mariners had staged an unlikely comeback against the most fabled club in pro baseball. The series was even at two games apiece, setting the stage for the most memorable moment in Washington sports history.

ALDS Game 5

The date was October 8, 1995. After an amazing stretch of September and October baseball, the city, the state, indeed the entire Northwest, had their eyes and ears glued to the Kingdome for Game 5 of the ALDS. If you were there, congratulations—you scored one of the toughest tickets to buy in the history of Seattle sports. Starting pitcher Andy Benes was decent through almost six innings, but the Mariners' bats were a little too quiet for comfort. The score was 4–2 Yankees in the eighth when Griffey Jr. stepped up to the plate and smacked out his fifth homer of the series to pull his team within a run of New York. After Griffey's homer, the Mariners loaded the bases, and Yankees starter David Cone walked Doug Strange to force in Tino Martinez and tie the score at 4–4. But that was all Seattle got that inning as Yankees manager Buck Showalter went to the bullpen for the team's sensational rookie, Mariano Rivera. Inning over.

After two Yankees reached bases in the ninth, Sweet Lou called on Randy Johnson from the bullpen. After only one day's rest, Johnson shut down the Yankees' rally with three straight outs. With Yankees starter Jack McDowell also pitching in relief, neither team scored in the 10th. But in the 11th, the Yankees got to Johnson with a run-scoring single by Randy Velarde. Johnson got enough strikeouts to end the inning, but the Mariners were down 5–4 heading into the bottom of the 11th.

Seattle went to work against McDowell with a perfect drag bunt for a base hit by Joey Cora. Then the crowd erupted at the sight of hot-hitting Griffey striding toward the plate. One swing and the game could be over. Griffey didn't hit one out, but he came up big nonetheless with a single to center field. On Griffey's hit, Cora rounded second base and moved safely to third. With two on and nobody out, the table was perfectly set for one Edgar Martinez, who had been blistering Yankees pitchers throughout the series. And he did it one more time, scorching a slider into left-center field, scoring Cora easily. But could Griffey score from first, or would he be stopped 90 feet away by Mariners third-base coach Sam Perlozzo? Rounding second base and picking up on Perlozzo, Griffey saw his third-base coach waving him home—frantically. Griffey rounded third, headed for home in full gallop, slid feet first and easily beat the relay to the plate. Score! Game! Series—Mariners! Seattle was on its way to the team's first-ever league championship series playoff.

The series' winning hit by Martinez ("Señor Octobre") set off a celebration on the field, in the grandstands and around the state. A joyous collision of ecstatic ballplayers at home plate quickly turned into the mother of all post-game pileups. At the bottom of this heap of humanity was a beaming Griffey—an image that represents the moment in time when more than a century of Seattle baseball made the quantum leap to the steps of baseball heaven. The dramatic, extra-inning series clincher galvanized a community and dismissed any lingering notion that the Mariners were leaving town. This team was and will always be the Seattle Mariners, and they weren't going to St. Petersburg—or anywhere else except to Cleveland to play the Indians for the right to go to the World Series.

Onto the ALCS

The Mariners pitchers were exhausted after the grueling series with the Yankees. With a bench full of tired arms, manager Piniella decided to go with late-season call-up Bob Wolcott as the team's starter in Game 1 of the American League Championship Series (ALCS) in Seattle. In the first inning, Wolcott pitched like you might expect a young, impressionable rookie to pitch in such a pressure-packed environment; he walked the first three batters to load the bases. But after a visit by Piniella—during which Wolcott was informed that with almost no options for long relievers, he was going to be on the mound for a while, no matter what happened that inning— the young pitcher did what seemed impossible against a heavy-hitting Cleveland lineup: he got out of the inning with no runs scored. With a two-run homer by Mike Blowers and a run-scoring double by Luis Sojo, the Mariners took Game 1. Wolcott pitched seven innings and picked up the win.

In Game 2 at the Kingdome, Piniella would only be so lucky to have a repeat Wolcott pitching performance. Seattle bats also went quiet against Orel Hershiser, and the Mariners dropped the contest 5–2. Finally with a rested starting pitcher ready for Game 3 in Cleveland, Piniella sent ace Randy Johnson to the mound. Johnson and his team entered the eighth inning leading 2–1 when Jay Buhner misplayed a fly ball to right field by Alvaro Espinoza, allowing an unearned run to tie the game at 2–2. But Buhner redeemed himself in a dramatic way with a three-run homer in the 11th to give the Mariners a win and the series lead at 2–1.

But with the Game 3 victory, the Mariners had pulled their last rabbit out of the hat—they lost both Games 4 and 5 in Cleveland. Back in Seattle for Game 6, Piniella called on his ace Johnson for yet another miracle. On only three days' rest, Johnson wasn't his sharpest, but he was good enough to keep the Mariners in the game until the eighth inning, trailing 1–0. However, with three more runs that inning, the Cleveland Indians were finally able to finish off the team that refused to lose. Final score: 4–0.

The end of the season had come for the Seattle Mariners and their fans, but nobody was in a hurry to leave the Kingdome. Some 15 minutes after the final out, word reached the Mariners clubhouse that the stadium wasn't emptying out. Amid a growing ovation, more than 57,000 fans refused to leave until they saw, one last time, the team that refused to lose. Fans got their encore when the team emerged back onto the field to a loud and heartfelt ovation that both shocked and touched many of the players.

Post-season Honors Aplenty

Early in his career, Randy Johnson was known as a pitcher with tons of speed but sometimes frightening (to batters, at least) control issues. Then, in 1992, Johnson was introduced to Nolan Ryan. The flame-throwing eight-time All-Star offered some tips that helped Johnson pitch with more control. That advice paid almost immediate dividends for Johnson who went 19–8 in 1993, his breakout year. In the Mariners' "refuse to lose" 1995 season, Johnson notched an 18–2 record and won the AL Cy Young Award. He remains the only Mariners pitcher to win the award. Piniella was also honored as AL Manager of the Year for the 1995 season.

Tall and Taller

Pitching ace Johnson is the tallest man to ever play in the majors. At six-feet-ten-inches tall, Johnson—aka, the Big Unit—looked more like eight-feet tall on top of the mound. Johnson channeled size and strength into a fastball that at times topped 100 miles per hour. On June 2, 1990, against the Detroit Tigers, Johnson was the first Mariners pitcher to throw a no-hitter. Playing with the Arizona Diamondbacks, the five-time Cy Young Award winner threw a perfect game in 2004 against the Atlanta Braves.

More on the Mariners...

Theory Disproved

Sometimes what went up at the Kingdome didn't always come down. Speakers hanging from the Kingdome ceiling were sometimes hit by pop-ups and foul balls, and on two occasions the balls didn't come down. Mariners center-fielder Rupert Jones caused the first incident in 1979, lodging a foul ball in the speaker above the first-base dugout. Milwaukee Brewer Ricky Nelson repeated the feat in 1983. Kingdome ground rules dictated strikes for each batter.

A Stadium Moon

Home-plate umpire Ted Hendry had been in the major leagues a long time and was one of the most respected men in the game—that is, until one particular game on April 13, 1980, when the Toronto Blue Jays traveled to Seattle to play against the Mariners.

Arriving at the ballpark hours before the start of the game, as per routine, Hendry went to the umpire dressing room to get into his uniform for the game. Instead of his older, worn uniform that he had donned for years, he found a clean, brand new uniform, fitted to his exact size. Although it was a little snug, Hendry managed to suck in his stomach and assume his position behind the plate.

Hendry could feel that the uniform was a tad too tight, but he had no choice other than to start the game. As the first batter approached the plate and Hendry bent down to call the pitch, the seam in the seat of his pants split wide open. Not only were his pants too tight, but his underwear also could not hold in his extra weight and split along with his pants, straight down the middle, exposing his rosy cheeks to all the unlucky fans in the expensive box seats behind the plate. To add to his misfortune, Hendry didn't even notice he was mooning the entire stadium. Blissfully unaware of his predicament, the show continued until the end of the inning when Hendry was politely and discreetly informed he was being an unwitting tease in front of the entire stadium.

Completely embarrassed, Hendry ran off to the dressing room for some quick repairs. A few minutes later, still red in the cheeks, he returned with only a safety pin holding his dignity in place. But when he bent over to start the next inning, the safety pin sprung open and poked him in the right buttock. Hendry let out a quiet yelp and bravely finished out the rest of the inning until he could return to the dressing room for further alterations.

Again he returned to the field with another safety pin holding his pants together, but when he bent down to call the next pitch, the newly placed safety pin flew open and the fans behind the plate began to roar with laughter. For six innings, Hendry stood at the plate with his behind hanging out of his pants. Finally, Seattle general manager Lou Gorman decided he had watched the umpire suffer enough and gave him a pair of blue shorts to put on under his torn pants. With the blue shorts blocking any further exposure, Hendry was able to finish out the game.

Blow, Blow, Blow

The Seattle Mariners' Lenny Randle definitely earns an "A" for effort for his attempt to bend the rules of baseball when trying to aid a ball across the foul line. The famous moment occurred during the sixth inning of a 1981 regular-season game between the Mariners and the visiting Kansas City Royals.

Kansas City outfielder Amos Otis was the first batter up in the inning. Swinging at the first pitch, Otis caught a piece of the ball with the end of his bat, sending the ball dribbling down the third-base line. Three Mariners players quickly surrounded the ball as it crept delicately along the edge of the foul line. They all figured the ball would be called a foul. But the ball stubbornly stayed on-side and Otis reached first base. Not wanting to simply allow the Kansas City player take the free hit, an idea came to the mind of Mariners third baseman Randle.

Dropping to his knees, Randle took a deep breath and blew as hard as he could on the ball. The entire stadium thought he had lost his marbles, but as they watched him puff up his cheeks and blow as hard as he could, the tactic actually began to work and the ball crossed the foul line.

Realizing that he was asking a lot of the umpire to allow the ball to be called foul, Randle immediately looked over to home-plate ump Larry McCoy, expecting him to wave at Otis to stay at first. But to everyone's surprise, McCoy signaled for Otis to return to home plate for another at-bat.

Without hesitation, Royals manager Jim Frey bounded out of the dugout and protested the called foul. After a few choice words from Frey and a brief conference with the other umpires, McCoy changed his call, and Otis was sent back to first base and given an infield hit. McCoy then explained to Randle that MLB rules clearly forbade players from altering the course of a ball in play.

In the dressing room after the game, Randle spoke to a crowd of reporters hungry for a quote about the incident.

"I didn't blow on it," he said with a wry smile. *"I used the power of suggestion. I was just telling the ball, 'Go foul, go foul.' The Bird* [Detroit pitcher Mark Fidrych] *used to talk to the ball, and he didn't get into any trouble. How could they call it a hit? It was a foul ball."*

Hard-hat Area

Like Fred Hutchinson, John Olerud was a local boy who made it to the major leagues. After leading his Interlake (Bellevue, Washington) High School baseball team to a 1986 state championship, Olerud headed to Washington State University in Pullman to play for the legendary Bobo Brayton just as his father, John Sr., had done more than 20 years earlier. At WSU, the younger Olerud became not only the best Cougars baseball player ever but also the best college baseball player in the country. Olerud could hit and pitch and did both for the Cougars. During his sophomore year, Olerud went 15–0 on the mound, hit .464 and was named the 1988 College Player of the Year. But then a brain aneurysm almost killed him in 1989. Treatment was successful, but Olerud never took the field again without his signature hard-shell baseball cap. Olerud became one of only a handful of players to go from the draft straight to the big leagues. At first base for most of his 17-season pro career, Olerud notched two World Series championships (both with the Toronto Blue Jays) and a 2001 All-Star game appearance in Seattle while playing with the Mariners, a dream come true for Olerud. He is also a 1993 Hutch Award recipient.

Mariner Moose Mishap

The Mariner Moose is the beloved symbol for the Mariners baseball franchise and can be seen at every home game doing anything he can to entertain the fans. But that zeal to keep the fans amused got the poor moose sent to the hospital during a game in 1995.

Well known for his love of burning through the field in his four-wheel off-road vehicle, the Mariner Moose decided to up the ante during the 1995 American League Division Series against the New York Yankees. Instead of riding on the ATV, the Mariner Moose thought it was a good idea to put on rollerblades and be towed by a long line. The driver of the ATV let the excitement of the playoffs get to him and went a little too fast, sending the Mariner Moose hurtling into the outfield wall. Instead of absorbing the impact with his body, the moose thought it was a good idea to let his feet stop him. Bad idea. The force of the impact broke his right ankle and he had to be carried off the field.

But the Mariner Moose's troubles on the ATV weren't over. During an August 2007 game versus the Boston Red Sox, the moose was up to his usual tricks in between innings, entertaining fans by speeding around the edge of the field. It's hard enough to steer an ATV at top speed on a well-manicured baseball field, but imagine doing it in a large foam mascot costume with a small mesh-covered window to see out of. A disaster was bound to happen. And so, on that sunny August day as the Mariner Moose sped his way around home plate, he failed to notice Red Sox player Coco Crisp, whose back was to the approaching ATV, warming up on the sidelines. Thankfully, at the last second, Crisp heard the warning screams from fans and fellow players in time to dive out of the way. It was a strange turn of events because a moose is usually the one staring down the grille of an oncoming vehicle.

Most Dingers

The illustrious distinction of hitting the most home runs as a team in one season does not belong to the New York Yankees or the Boston Red Sox but to the 1997 Seattle Mariners. The Mariners had the hot bats that year, blasting out 264 home runs during the regular season. The only team to come close to beating that record was the 2000 Houston Astros who managed 249 home runs. In 1997, Griffey Jr. led the team with 56 home runs, followed by Jay Buhner with 40, Paul Sorrento with 31 and Alex Rodriguez with 23. The 1997 season was definitely another good year to be a Mariners fan.

Magic Season, Somber End

In 2001, the Mariners took on a whole new dynamic with the signing of right-fielder Ichiro Suzuki, the first Japanese position player to land a job in major-league baseball. He was also, by the way, a pretty good hitter. Suzuki was the first player since Jackie Robinson to lead the majors in both average (.350) and steals (56), and won both the 2001 AL MVP and Rookie of the Year awards.

With strong pitching—including a lights-out bullpen—Lou Piniella and the Mariners won an AL record 116 games in 2001, which tied the 1906 Chicago Cubs' all-time major-league record for wins. It was the team's third AL West title and marked the first time in franchise history that the Mariners reached the playoffs in consecutive seasons (they made it in 2000 as a wild card). Piniella picked up another AL Manager of the Year award for his efforts in 2001, and in the same season, Jamie Moyer also became the Mariners' second 20-game winner. But interestingly enough, while the Mariners sent eight players to the 2001 All-Star game, hosted by Seattle that year, Moyer wasn't one of those players.

Like in the storied 1995 playoffs, the Indians and Yankees stood in the way of a coveted Mariners World Series appearance in 2001. But Seattle was loaded with talent—surely this was going to be the season. In the five-game ALDS, Seattle, ominously, needed to rally from two games back to dispatch Cleveland. Against the Yankees in the ALCS, the Mariners managed only a single win (Game 3), and dropped the seven-game series— along with what was thought to be their best shot ever at the World Series—in only five games. After a record-setting run through the 2001 season, coming up short of the World Series left fans feeling slighted. Only one other team in major-league history has won more than 105 games and not made it to the World Series (the Atlanta Braves in 1998).

For most Mariners fans, though, the 2001 season isn't remembered for the playoff letdown. It's remembered for the way the team celebrated on the field the night they beat the California Angels 5–0 to clinch their third AL West title.

The day was Wednesday, September 19. Eight days had passed since the 9/11 terrorist attacks. Major League Baseball had only resumed play two nights before the Mariners/Angels game. Mindful and respectful of the somber mood across the country, the Mariners didn't jump for joy or dog-pile at home plate after the final pop-out to Bret Boone. Instead, they lined up—as was custom after their wins—to exchange high-fives and handshakes. Then the team gathered around the pitcher's mound—coaches, Piniella, everybody—and knelt before an American flag held high by Mariners third baseman Mark McLemore. The stadium crowd of 45,000 grew quiet and joined the Mariners for a moment of silence. For many fans and players—who wrestled with the idea of participating in an event so trivial in light of the grim national tragedy a little more than a week earlier—it was a powerful tribute. It was a moment everyone in the stadium needed, a moment in which a diverse set of fans, players, coaches and stadium vendors united in their one common bond: they were American, standing as friends, standing as one, remembering the fallen and drawing on the power of silence and unity to move on.

Following the emotional moment around the mound, the team proceeded to take the American flag on a march around the stadium. Amid growing cheers, the team finally landed at home plate where Piniella took the flag and hoisted it high one last time before the memorable and respectful tribute was finished.

Ichiro Heats Up

As remarkable as his 2001 season was, Ichiro Suzuki had just scratched the surface of a (no doubt) hall-of-fame career. On Friday, October 1,

2004, Suzuki broke George Sisler's long-standing single-season hits record of 257 set in 1920 with the St. Louis Browns. Who was the unlucky pitcher to toss the sinker-ball on a 3–2 count to Suzuki? Ryan Drese of the Texas Rangers. Suzuki slapped a grounder by the shortstop, setting a new single-season hits record of 258. He pushed the record higher with every hit during the rest of the season, ultimately setting the record at 262. That year, Suzuki was presented with the commissioner's Historic Achievement Award and is one of only eight recipients—ever.

The 2006 season represented the sixth straight year in which Suzuki recorded 200 or more hits. Only two other players in major-league history have accomplished that feat—Willie Keeler (1894–1901) and Wade Boggs (1983–89). By the end of the 2009 season, Ichiro had logged nine consecutive 200-hit seasons (despite not playing for the first eight games in 2009 because of a bleeding ulcer), surpassing Keeler's all-time record of eight. Suzuki also made nine consecutive All-Star game appearances and won nine Gold Glove awards for the Mariners.

A Few Good Men

Former Seattle Mariners third baseman and designated hitter Edgar Martinez was one of the most consistent hitters in all of professional baseball.

Upon retirement in 2004, Martinez joined Ted Williams, Babe Ruth, Stan Musial, Rogers Hornsby, Lou Gehrig, Manny Ramirez and Todd Helton as the only players in history with 300 home runs, 500 doubles, a career batting average higher than .300, a career on-base percentage higher than .400 and a career slugging percentage higher than .500.

The Ones Who Got Away

The Mariners never seem to have problems with finding talent. It's figuring out a way to keep it that has dogged the franchise to the point of lore. You could field a remarkable All-Star team with former Mariners—both major- and minor-leaguers—whose best years came after leaving Seattle: Randy Johnson, Alex Rodriguez, Tino Martinez, Omar Vizquel, Raul Ibanez, Adam Jones, Ryan Franklin, Jason Varitek and Ken Griffey Jr. (though, many will argue Griffey's best years came when he played for the Mariners from 1989 to 1999). After nine years in Cincinnati (and a brief stint with the Chicago White Sox), Junior returned to Seattle in 2009 to play once again for the Mariners.

A-Rod's Not-so-welcome Home

While Griffey's trips to Seattle as a Reds player saw warm reunions between a beloved former player and Mariners fans, visits by former Mariners shortstop Alex Rodriguez as a Texas Ranger and then a New York Yankee saw just the opposite. Seattle fans felt spurned by A-Rod's departure in 2003—an exit, most believed, that was fueled solely by the lure of a bigger contract. It is hard to argue otherwise. Rodriguez signed a 10-year, $252-million contract with the Texas Rangers, by far the largest contract in all of professional sports history at that time. Owner Tom Hicks paid less than that amount ($250 million) for the entire Rangers franchise just three years earlier. A-Rod's deal surpassed that of Ken Griffey Jr.'s, whose nine-year, $116.5-million deal with the Reds was a record (in 2003) for baseball contracts. Griffey, however, was welcome in Seattle, and the city's friendly receptions toward him were big factors in his decision to rejoin the Mariners in 2009.

Actors at Bat

Playing shortstop on the San Bernardino Inland Empire 66ers minor-league team in 2003, actor Kevin Costner went hitless in an exhibition game against the Seattle Mariners. When Costner made the move to the pitcher's mound late in the game, Mariners manager Lou Piniella inserted himself into the lineup. Costner walked him.

It wasn't Piniella's first experience with actors posing as baseball players. In 1991, Tom Selleck was facing Piniella's Cincinnati Reds when the manager grew tired of the actor's long plate appearance. Piniella instructed pitcher Tim Layana to throw heat at the batter and get him out. Selleck fouled off a few pitches but eventually struck out.

French Fries for Baseball

Some teams have rally hats, the Mariners have rally fries. A relatively new tradition, rally fries began during a 2007 home game against the Cincinnati Reds when an overeager fan tried, with one bare hand and the other holding a basket of fries, to catch a foul ball along the right-field line. The fan missed the ball and ended up spilling his fries all over the field. Mariners broadcaster and former player Mike Blowers noticed and suggested to his on-air partner Dave Sims that they send a new basket of fries to the man. The two broadcasters agreed and had a basket of fries delivered to the surprised fan. All of this was caught on television, and at the next game, fans made signs asking Bowers and Sims for free fries, requests to which they complied. Coincidentally, every time the fries were sent out, the Mariners seemed to score or rally from behind to win the game, and thus "rally fries" were created. Since that day in 2007, Mariners fans continually try to create the most elaborate signs and wear the strangest costumes to get Blowers' attention for their free fries, and until the Mariners stop rallying from behind to win, the fries continue to be sent out.

Working for Peanuts

Sure, his peanuts are always warm and perfectly roasted, but it's the way the Peanut Man delivers his snacks that has delighted Mariners fans for four decades. Rick Kaminski is a stadium peanut vendor with a strong arm and uncanny control. Early in his career, Kaminski started tossing his orders to fans to hurry up sales, and his talent for airmailing peanuts to fans—overhand or behind the back, and always right on target—eventually earned him a celebrity status that rose above some of the Mariners players themselves. So popular is Kaminski that he spends nearly a quarter of his time in the stadium signing autographs.

Closet Still Full

One more closing fact about the Mariners: after more than 33 seasons, and all the antics and great players who have passed through the roster, the Seattle Mariners have yet to retire a jersey number.

Chapter Two

Touchdown, Seahawks!

In the 1960s, officials from the city of Seattle, King County and the state were doubly motivated to get a new stadium built, not only to accommodate major-league baseball but also pro football. Indeed, the National Football League was sending strong signals that Seattle would be, could be, might be an attractive expansion market—if the city could muster a stadium fit for pro football. With the successful Forward Thrust stadium initiative in 1968, up went the Kingdome (though not exactly lickety-split!), and on December 5, 1974, the NFL awarded an expansion franchise to Seattle where retail magnate Lloyd Nordstrom (of the Nordstrom clothing-store chain) was ready and willing to pay the expansion fee and build the team. Sadly, Nordstrom never saw his team play. He died from a heart attack in January 1976.

Build It and They Will, Well...You Know...

While the franchise was at work immediately assembling coaches, finding a name for the team and choosing players, construction crews were busy putting the finishing touches on a new multi-purpose stadium: the Kingdome. Nearly two decades in the making, the giant concrete structure was finally taking shape just south of downtown Seattle. The unique indoor stadium represented more than a place where pro football and baseball (and at times, pro basketball) teams could share the turf; it also represented a coming of age for a city that had long sought to be a major market player on the national stage, and nothing signaled elite status (at least in the 1960s and 1970s) like major-league sports. By the mid-1970s, Seattle had landed the big three: the NFL, MLB and the NBA. Seattle had arrived.

Breaking in the 'Dome

Seattle's new NFL franchise wasn't the first team to play a game in the Kingdome—and neither were the Mariners. The distinction of that first game went to the Seattle Sounders of the North American Soccer League. Before more than 58,000 fans, the Sounders broke in the "'Dome" against the New York Cosmos on April 25, 1976. Less than a month later, minister Billy Graham packed 74,000 into the new stadium—an attendance that turned out to be the largest crowd the Kingdome ever saw. Also, touring America for the first time since 1966 with The Beatles, Paul McCartney, with his group Wings, staged the first-ever rock concert at the Kingdome on June 10, 1976.

So, What Is a Seahawk, Anyway?

Seattle's football team got its name by a fan ballot. The name "Seahawks" won with more than 1700 votes. A seahawk is an osprey, a large raptor that feeds primarily on fish. The Seahawks emblem is based on the Haida tribal design of a bald eagle, and the team's cheerleaders are called the Sea Gals.

Signing a Defensive Genius, Even if he is a Duck

The Seahawks' first coach was former University of Oregon Ducks football great Jack Patera. In the 1960s and 1970s, Patera was considered one of the NFL's best defensive coaches. He had put together the "Fearsome Foursome" defensive line while coaching with the Los Angeles Rams, then later formed the Minnesota Vikings' famed defensive front known as "Purple People Eaters."

A First Time for Everything

Two new NFL teams came into the league in 1976: the Seattle Seahawks and the Tampa Bay

Buccaneers. The Seattle Seahawks played their first regulation NFC West game on September 12, 1976, against the St. Louis Cardinals, a 30–24 loss. The new franchise didn't win until their sixth game of the season, overtaking their expansion brethren, the Tampa Bay Buccaneers, on the road, 13–10. The date was October 17. The first win at the Kingdome came three weeks later against the Atlanta Falcons, 30–13. The team and fans tasted victory only twice that year, going 2–12 in their inaugural season.

The One Who Got Away

Moved to the American Football Conference (AFC) West in their second season, the 1977 Seattle Seahawks showed some improvement over the 2–12 team of '76, going 5–9. The wins included the first-ever Seahawks shutout (17–0) in a victory against the Jets in New York. But the year is remembered by a dubious team move that occurred before the season even started. The Seahawks held the second overall pick of the 1977 draft and wanted to take Pittsburgh's Heisman Trophy–winning running back Tony Dorsett. The problem was that Dorsett had made it widely known that he didn't want to play in Seattle. The Seahawks were boxed into a corner and decided to trade their pick to Dallas for the 14th overall pick and three second-round picks. On the surface, it appeared that Dallas got the better part of the deal, but it actually ended up working out for Seattle as well—the team ultimately landed six players who started more than 300 games for the Seahawks. None of the players acquired in the trade were marquee names (guard Steve August, tackle Tom Lynch and linebacker Terry Beeson among them), but they were good players nonetheless, and the Seahawks managed a 9–7 record in only their third year in the league. Jack Patera was also named the 1978 NFL Coach of the Year.

Small College Wonder

When David Krieg stepped onto the Seahawks practice field for the first time in 1980, he didn't exactly bring with him a big-time college-football résumé. As an undrafted free-agent from tiny Milton College (which closed in 1982) in Wisconsin, Krieg was perhaps the ultimate NFL long shot. But, by the end of the 1981 season, he was the Seahawks' starting quarterback. With Pro-Bowl running back Curt Warner and future Hall of Fame receiver Steve Largent as receiver, Krieg led the Seahawks to their first playoff appearance in 1983 that produced the epic upset of the Miami Dolphins. Krieg left the team in 1992 and went on to play for five other NFL teams before retiring at the end of the 1998 season. Krieg's career passing statistics put him in the top 10 in many categories—right along with many legends of the game, including John Elway, Warren Moon, Dan Fouts and Joe Montana. Among Krieg's many Seahawks records is most consecutive games with a touchdown pass (28). Not bad for a guy who started his college career as the seventh-string quarterback (can you get any lower in the depth chart?) at a school that doesn't exist anymore.

Zorn to Largent

Despite Krieg's success, far and away the most beloved Seattle Seahawks player is receiver Steve Largent, the team's first Pro Bowler. Indeed, the phrase "Zorn to Largent" (as in, quarterback Jim Zorn throwing to receiver Largent) became so commonplace in Seahawks sports lexicon that it came to connote the very essence of team success in the early days of the franchise (yes, there were successes in the early days of the franchise, including the aforementioned 9–7 season in only the team's third year). At five-feet-eleven-inches and 187 pounds, Largent wasn't large or fast, but he had sure hands, a knack for getting open and he played with quarterbacks who knew how to find him. So prolific was the Zorn to Largent hookup (and later, the Krieg to Largent hookup) that Largent held virtually all of the NFL's major receiving records by the time of his retirement— including a then-record 177 consecutive games with a catch, most receptions in a career (819) and most touchdown receptions (100).

Back at 'Cha, Pal

Despite his pass-catching prowess, one of Largent's most memorable plays came not by a catch, but by a tackle. In a 1988 game against the Denver Broncos, Largent was blasted hard after a catch by safety Mike Harden. Largent lost a few teeth in the hit he thought was illegal. Later in the season, the Broncos were visitors in the Kingdome. Harden intercepted a David Krieg pass and was racing back upfield when suddenly, out of nowhere, Largent blasted Harden—a legal hit that flattened him to the turf and caused him to fumble the ball, which Largent recovered. The crowd went crazy at the score-settling play.

Do Not Disturb

In 1989, the Seattle Seahawks established the Steve Largent Award—given to a team member who best exemplifies the spirit, dedication and integrity of the famed player. And the first winner of the award? Steve Largent. Also in 1989, Largent completed his 100th touchdown catch (December 10) and was the only Seahawks player on the roster to have played in the team's first game in 1976. Largent was inducted into the Pro Football Hall of Fame in 1995, was the first

Seahawk to have his number retired and he eventually became a congressman representing the state of Oklahoma. Largent's number 80 jersey, however, was taken out of retirement in 2004 when the team acquired receiver Jerry Rice, who wore the number during his prolific years with the San Francisco 49ers. Largent had agreed to the use of his number, but fans had not. Controversy ensued over whose "big idea" it was to reuse such a sacred jersey. Rice said at the time that it was Seahawks officials who first suggested it.

A Jersey and a Ring for Pete's Sake

Every team needs a voice, and for the Seattle Seahawks' first 17 years as a team that voice belonged to Pete Gross. A familiar voice to the state from his days as the University of Washington football and basketball play-by-play announcer, Gross teamed up with University of Washington Huskies legend Don Heinrich for the original Seahawks broadcasts before the team's receiver, Steve Raible, retired from play and joined the broadcast team. Gross endeared himself to legions of Seahawks fans because of his enthusiastic style and trademark "Touchdown, Seahawks!" call line.

Gross lost a kidney to cancer during the 1989 Seahawks season. That was the same year Largent broke a 44-year-old NFL record for touchdown catches (100). It was one of the more high-profile

NFL records to be broken, and the jersey Largent wore during that game against Cincinnati was certain to be shipped off to the Hall of Fame. But in a surprise move, Largent gave his jersey to a stunned Gross.

In 1992, Gross received another accolade: an induction into the Seahawks Ring of Honor. During the induction ceremony at halftime of a Monday night game against the Denver Broncos, Gross delivered one last "Touchdown, Seahawks!" to the cheers of his adoring fans in the Kingdome. Two days later, he died of cancer.

Fitting Memorial

While undergoing cancer treatment at centers around the country, Gross noted a distinct lack of appropriate, affordable temporary housing for cancer patients often traveling far from home seeking care. Following his death, Gross' family teamed up with the Fred Hutchinson Cancer Research Center and other Seattle businesses to establish the Pete Gross House that now provides safe, clean, affordable housing for cancer patients who are not from Seattle.

Finally, Some Real Success

The Seahawks' first taste of playoff action came in 1983 in only the first year under veteran NFL coach Chuck Knox. Seattle parlayed a 9–7 record into a wildcard playoff spot against Denver, blowing past the Broncos 31–7 to face the Miami Dolphins in an epic divisional playoff game. Few people gave the Seahawks a chance against a heavily favored 12–4 Dolphins team whose rookie quarterback, Dan Marino, was having a stellar season—not just for a rookie but for any NFL quarterback. The Seahawks, however, were confident behind their own (underrated and underappreciated) quarterback David Krieg, even when they were trailing in the fourth quarter.

With a little more than three minutes left in the game, the Seattle Seahawks drove down the field—with key completions along the way to Largent—and scored on a two-yard Curt Warner dive into the end zone. The score was 24–20, with 1:48 seconds to play. Then, in a stunning development before a disbelieving Orange Bowl crowd, the Dolphins fumbled away their last-chance possession. With a late field goal, Seattle won the game 27–20 in what is considered to be one of the greatest NFL upsets of all time. Seahawks players hoisted Coach Knox onto their shoulders and gave him a ride across the field. With the win, he became the first NFL coach to win division titles with three different teams (the Seattle Seahawks, Buffalo Bills and L.A. Rams).

Alas, the Seahawks couldn't take that last step to make it to the Super Bowl, losing 30–14 to the Los Angeles Raiders in the AFC Championship game the next week. But Seahawks fans knew they had a winner in their first-year coach and were completely on board with his "Ground Chuck" (running-style) offense.

At 12–4, Knox was named the 1984 Coach of the Year, but in the 1985 season he couldn't get his team past the Dolphins in a divisional playoff rematch, losing 31–10. In fact, the Seahawks didn't win another playoff game for more than 20 years.

A Dark Chapter

While the Seahawks' offense finally got some traction in the early 1980s, the Seattle defense also had a star in Kenny Easley. With his penchant for pickoffs, Easley was the 1981 AFC Defensive Rookie of the Year, 1983 AFC Defensive Player of the year and 1984 NFL Defensive Player of the Year—not to mention a five-time Pro Bowler. Needless to say, Easley was a huge fan favorite. So when he was traded in 1998 to the Phoenix Cardinals, people were not happy. The story grew darker when the trade was canceled after Easley failed his physical with the Cardinals. Turns out Easley had kidney problems—serious ones. With full-blown kidney failure, Easley's playing days were over and he eventually underwent a successful kidney transplant.

Easley sued the Seahawks, claiming that heavy doses of the ibuprofen he'd taken for an ankle injury had caused the kidney damage, and that the team trainers and doctors should have known better. The two parties, along with the drug maker of the ibuprofen, eventually settled out of court. But it was a sad and contentious moment for the beloved former Seahawk and the franchise itself. In time, though, the Seahawks took a step toward making things right. In 2002, Easley was inducted into his rightful place in the Seahawks Ring of Honor.

12 Men on the Field

With its cavernous feel, the Kingdome was not the greatest stadium in all of football, but it did have some advantages. Because of its concrete dome, sound waves didn't really have anywhere to escape and therefore reverberated around the stadium. This was an annoying problem for stadium announcers but a blessing for the Seahawks. Whenever an opposing team had possession of the football, the fans got so loud that quarterbacks could not be heard when calling signals or changing plays at the line of scrimmage. Other teams had loud fans, too, but nothing could compare to the ear-shattering racket of the

Seahawks' faithful. When the decibel level was measured, Seahawks fans were as noisy as a jumbo jet's engines. The tremendous din resulted in so many false starts, penalties and blown plays by the opposition that players and media often referred to Seahawks fans as the 12th man on the field. In 1984, in honor of the fans, the number 12 was actually retired by the Seahawks.

Things did not change when the Seahawks moved to Qwest Field. From 2005 to the end of the 2008 season, the fans caused a league-leading 78 false-start penalties. In a sport where the outcome of a game can be decided by a few yards, any team would welcome that kind of statistic. And so, in honor of the fans' continuing contribution to the team's success, before every home game, a 12th-man flag is ceremoniously raised at the south end of the stadium.

12th Man Nearly Sacked

Claiming trademark infringement, Texas A&M University filed a lawsuit in 2006 that, if successful, would have prevented the Seahawks from referring to the 12th man at games or in marketing materials. The university owned a copyright to the term and was ready to protect it, even in court, if necessary. (Well, excuse me!) Fortunately, the two sides struck an agreement in which the Seahawks acknowledged that the school owned the copyright, and from then forward paid a fee to the university to use the term.

Talk about Promoting from Within

The Seahawks' executive vice president of football operations from 1995 to 1999 was Randy Mueller. But it wasn't Mueller's first job with the Seahawks. In the late 1970s, Mueller was a local high school kid working the sidelines as the Seahawks' ball boy. He left the team to quarterback Linfield College in McMinnville, Oregon, to a 1982 National Association of Intercollegiate Athletics (NAIA) Division II Championship. The small-college football hero then returned to the Seahawks, but this time in the front office as personnel assistant. Two promotions later, Mueller was a VP.

The Doctor Is In

Seahawks playoff MVP in 1983 and former WSU Cougar Dan Dornick studied more than the playbook during his NFL career; he also studied medicine. Teammates called him Dr. Dan. After retiring from the NFL, Dornick finished his medical studies and became a real doctor—in Yakima, Washington.

Center of Attention

Another WSU Cougar-turned-Seahawk was Robbie Tobeck. The center started his NFL career as an undrafted rookie in 1994 with the Atlanta Falcons and joined the Seahawks in 2000. In 2005, Tobeck was the first (and still only) Seahawk center to be named to the Pro Bowl.

Iron Man

Seahawks defensive tackle Joe Nash gets the Iron Man award for having appeared in the most Seahawks games—218. Nash played his entire career in Seattle—15 years, from 1982 to 1996.

Touch and Go

The first time Seahawk rookie running back Curt Warner touched the ball for his new team in 1983, he sprinted 60 yards for a touchdown. Warner led the league in rushing that year and was named to the Pro Bowl. Now a Vancouver, Washington, resident, Warner was added to the Seahawks Ring of Honor in 1994.

The Boz, Bo and Mr. Ed

Brian Keith Bosworth—"The Boz." Where do you start with this guy? How about at college, where Bosworth was a smart student with crazy haircuts and a two-time winner of the Butkus Award while playing linebacker for the Oklahoma

Sooners. Early in his college career in Oklahoma, Bosworth and his Sooners lost to the University of Washington Huskies (28–17) in the 1984 Orange Bowl, a game remembered for the infamous Sooner Schooner incident in which Oklahoma was assessed a 15-yard penalty when their Sooner wagon didn't get off the field quick enough. Throughout all of this, many thought Bosworth had done enough to launch a successful career at the next level, but it was not so cut-and-dried— Bosworth had a personality trait that didn't serve him well: he was a loudmouth. Banned by the NCAA from playing in the 1987 Orange Bowl for steroid use, Bosworth defiantly wore a T-shirt on the sideline that said "National Communists Against Athletes." Nevertheless, Bosworth was considered one of the greatest college football players ever, and expectations for his pro career were off the charts.

Ahead of the draft, Bosworth sent letters to several NFL teams for whom he would not play if selected. As one of the teams that did not receive his letter, the Tacoma Stars chose Bosworth—in the Major Indoor Soccer League draft of 1987. It was a joke, of course—a light-hearted jab at Bosworth's arrogance. Fortunately (or unfortunately?) the Seahawks didn't get a letter either and took Bosworth in the supplemental draft. Bosworth arrived in Seattle amid a media frenzy the likes of which the town hadn't seen before. Bosworth signed a then-Seahawk record 10-year, $11-million contract and was delivered to his first practice by helicopter. Before the regular season even started, Bosworth sued the NFL for the right to wear his college number 44 jersey. He lost the suit and was assigned number 55. When it finally came time to play games, The Boz was actually decent—if not terrific at times— using his trademark speed and strength with no small amount of arrogance to become one of the most targeted players in the NFL by both players and fans. Prior to a game against Denver, Bosworth famously referred to Broncos QB John Elway as "Mr. Ed." Broncos fans in turn greeted the Seahawks with "Boz Buster" T-shirts that turned out to be shirts manufactured by Bosworth's own company. Some years later, it was learned that the entire Bosworth persona (bad guy on the field, good guy off...though not much is remembered about the "good guy off" part) was a marketing scheme cooked up by The Boz and his agent.

One of the most lasting memories many fans have of Brian Bosworth is that of him getting plowed over at the goal line by Oakland Raiders running back Bo Jackson (but then, Jackson plowed over a lot of players in his career). In that same Monday night game, Jackson broke a 91-yard run for a touchdown with Bosworth chasing, but unable to catch, the running back down the sideline. Jackson kept running through the end zone and disappeared into the Kingdome locker-room tunnel for a few seconds before re-emerging in front of a stunned crowd.

Aside from having people angry with him, Bosworth's biggest and most serious problem as a pro athlete was his inability to stay healthy. Shoulder injuries limited The Boz to only three years of NFL action. Thanks for the memories, just the same.

After football, Bosworth turned to acting but has only a handful of movies to his credit. More recently, he has been selling real estate in the Los Angeles area.

My Way or the Highway

In yet another draft quandary, the Seahawks held the 16th overall pick in the 1991 NFL draft. Team officials agreed that the pick was to be spent on a quarterback, but which one? Owner Ken Behring was adamant about grabbing San Diego State QB Dan McGwire, younger brother of slugger Mark McGwire of baseball's St. Louis Cardinals. Seahawks coach Chuck Knox didn't think much of Dan McGwire, insisting that other QBs were worthy of consideration, including a kid from the University of Southern Mississippi named Brett Favre. Behring pulled rank and the team selected McGwire, who promptly became one of the NFL's biggest busts, playing in only a few games over five years. Knox resigned at the end of the 1991 season, and by the end of the 1992 season under new coach Tom Flores, the Seahawks hit a new low with a team-record 14 losses against only two wins.

I Know Joe Montana, and You're no Joe Montana

The 1993 draft was also well stocked with quarterbacks, and the Seahawks held the second overall pick. Two seemingly can't-miss choices faced the team: Notre Dame's Rick Mirer and Washington State's Drew Bledsoe. Supposedly the "next Joe Montana," Mirer was chosen by the Seahawks after the New England Patriots selected Bledsoe, despite an obvious preference by Seattle fans for the opposite scenario. Turns out, Mirer was no Joe Montana (not even a distant cousin), never lived up to expectations and was traded to the Chicago Bears before the 1997 season. Bledsoe went on to have a stellar career with New England and led the Patriots to a Super Bowl appearance in 1996, losing 35–21 to a Mike Holmgren–coached Green Bay Packer team with, you guessed it, Brett Favre at quarterback.

Listen to a Story 'bout a Man Named Ken

From 1977 to 1999, the Seattle Seahawks and the Seattle Mariners had a common bond (or perhaps, a common Achilles heel): the Kingdome. By the 1990s, the concrete superstructure was hated as much as it was beloved in the late 1970s. Aside from the crumbling, aging facility (in such a state after only two decades, not that old by stadium standards), the Seahawks of the mid-1990s grew tired of sharing their stadium with pro baseball. Around the NFL and in Major League Baseball, stadiums were being built for exclusive tenants—replete with modern amenities and money-making suites that franchises coveted. Seahawks owner Ken Behring was no different in that regard—he wanted out of the 'Dome.

Not convinced the county (which actually owned the stadium) could affect the necessary repairs and upgrades, Behring loaded up the trucks and moved to Beverly—Hills, that is. Or he came close to moving, anyway. In February 1996, Behring attempted to set up shop at the vacated Rams Park in Anaheim (the Rams had departed a year earlier to St. Louis), but the facility was closed for remodeling so Behring's equipment was just off-loaded and stored in the cafeteria. Not for long...

NFL commissioner Paul Tagliabue wasn't supportive of Behring's off-season, end-around play. And when King County Executive Gary Locke won a restraining order that stated the Seahawks could play only in the Kingdome, the trucks turned around and headed back to Seattle. Nice try, Ken.

Between Behring's meddling in the trenches of team operations and his attempt to move the franchise to California, he isn't remembered by most fans as a favorite owner of the Seahawks.

The County Football Factory

After a stellar college coaching career, Everett, Washington, native Dennis Erickson took over as Seahawks head coach in 1995. Erickson was born in Washington and graduated from Everett High School, class of 1965. Dennis' father, "Pink" Erickson, was a renowned high school coach at Everett's Cascade High School while his son played football at rival Everett High School, which was coached by the Ericksons' next-door neighbor, Bill Dunn. In his junior year, Dennis beat out future Cougars head football coach, Mike Price, for the starting QB job. Erickson also coached the Cougars (1987–88) before Price (1989–2002), and recommended his old high school teammate for the Cougars job when he vacated Washington State for a head coaching job at the University of Miami. Erickson notched two college national championships with Miami, but in what was maybe an omen of things to come, the school ended up saddled with three years of probation due to NCAA rule violations by the time Erickson departed in 1995 for his Seahawks job.

Upon Further Review

Erickson's dubious karma followed him right back to the Puget Sound where, before he even coached his first game, police arrested him for drunk driving on the Interstate 5 in Snohomish County. And then, in his first three seasons with the Seahawks, the team never finished better than .500. Overall, in four seasons as head coach, Erickson never posted a better record than 8–8. But in 1998 (Erickson's final year as coach), the team just missed the playoffs on what many fans believe was a blown call by the officials. In New York against the Jets, quarterback Vinny Testaverde was attempting a fourth-down sneak into the end zone with seconds left in the game but appeared to come up a yard short of the goal line. Surprisingly, line judge Ernie Frantz signaled a touchdown. Television replays seemed to confirm that Testaverde was short—way short. However, in 1998, instant replays were not used by NFL officials, so the touchdown stood. The Seahawks lost 32–31, missed the playoffs that season by one game and Erickson was finished as coach of the team. Not coincidentally, many believe, the use of instant replays to settle disputed or close calls by game officials was reinstituted by the NFL the next season.

The Mother of all Local Owners

Tired of Seattle and tired of the Kingdome, Ken Behring sold his Seahawks franchise in 1997 for $200 million to Microsoft co-founder Paul Allen. One of the wealthiest men in the world, Allen brought financial stability to the franchise and promised to keep it in Seattle with the construction of a new football and soccer stadium. He also contributed $130 million to the $430-million stadium-and-events-center budget. Allen, a WSU dropout, also owns the Portland Trailblazers and part of the Seattle Sounders MLS club—among dozens (if not hundreds) of other holdings. In 1999, Allen also bought the best football coach he could find, wrestling Mike Holmgren away from the Green Bay Packers.

Recycle, Recycle

But before the new Seahawks Stadium could go up, the old one had to come down. To great fanfare, and virtually no opposition, the Kingdome was imploded at the young age of 24 on March 26, 2000. At the time, it was the world's largest implosion of a single concrete structure. Much of the rubble from the Kingdome was recycled, and about half of it was used for the new stadium. The Seahawks played the 2000 and 2001 seasons at Husky Stadium while their new stadium was being built where the Kingdome once stood. Seahawks Stadium opened in 2002 (naming rights were later sold to Qwest Communications, thus the current name of Qwest Field), and in two years the Seahawks went from playing in one of the ugliest venues in pro football to boasting one of the most beautiful open-air stadiums in the league. Seating capacity is listed at just above 67,000 with 70 percent of those seats covered by a 210,000-square-foot roof. Field-level luxury suites in the Seahawks Stadium were also the first of their kind in the NFL.

Super Seahawks

Allen and team president Bob Whitsitt hoped the new stadium would turn the team into a Super Bowl contender, but it wasn't meant to be during the first season in the new stadium when the Seahawks went 7–9. The 2002 year also saw the team move back to the NFC, where, if you remember, they originally started out.

Impressive Résumé, Mr. ...Holmgren, Is it?

With the hiring of Mike Holmgren in 1999, there were high hopes that the new coach would engineer the same remarkable turnaround in Seattle as he had in Green Bay. After all, prior to his arrival on the "frozen tundra," the Packers were perennial losers. By the time Holmgren left, his coaching stint was considered among the best in NFL history, having taken the Packers to two Super Bowls (winning Super Bowl XXXI), setting records for post-season victories and establishing a regular-season win/loss record of 75–37. Talk about a killer résumé! With such an excellent work history, Seahawks brass made Holmgren not just coach but also general manager.

Ending a Decade-long Drought

Holmgren delivered the goods in his first season, leading the Seahawks to an AFC West division title and their first playoff appearance in 10 years. But the coach and team tripped and missed the play-offs for the next three seasons. Holmgren was "relieved" of his general manager duties so he could focus on coaching, and the move paid off with a post-season appearance as an NFC Wild Card team in 2003.

A Seahawks Rarity

With the Seahawks' Holmgren era gaining traction (a good thing, because his seat was getting a little toasty), the team won the NFC West in 2005 with the league's best offense and a franchise-best 13–3 record. Seahawks running back Shaun Alexander had the legs, too, cranking out 1880 yards during his MVP season. And then, in the divisional playoffs, Seattle did something they hadn't done in 21 years: win a playoff game. The Seahawks bested the Washington Redskins 20–10 in the hard-fought, monumental game. The 12th man was delirious.

In the NFC Championship game, the Seahawks jumped out to an early lead on the Carolina Panthers and never looked back, winning easily, 34–14. The 12th man never roared so loud and more joyously. The Seattle Seahawks had earned their first-ever Super Bowl appearance. This was Holmgren's third Super Bowl, and with it, he became one of only five coaches in league history to take two different NFL franchises to the Super Bowl.

The Seahawks and Super Bowl XL

The Seattle Seahawks rolled into Detroit for Super Bowl XL on February 6, 2006. Playing against the Pittsburgh Steelers, the Seahawks were cast as spoilers to the warm and fuzzy thought of Steelers running back Jerome Bettis returning to his hometown for a happy ending to his career. The Seahawks could care less about their opponent's impending retirement and gave the Steelers a pretty good go of it. In fact, Seattle looked to be taking the lead on a Matt Hasselbeck to Darrell Jackson touchdown pass in the second quarter. Officials ruled the receiver out of bounds; replays showed otherwise. And, just a few plays earlier, Steelers QB Ben Roethlisberger had been awarded a touchdown despite replays that showed the football never crossed the goal line. Indeed, Seattle was feeling snake-bit by poor officiating. There was more to come.

In the fourth quarter, Hasselbeck threw an interception to Pittsburgh's Ike Taylor. During the return, the Seahawks QB hit a Pittsburgh player too low, in the opinion of the officials, and Hasselbeck was flagged for unsportsmanlike conduct. The NFL later admitted that the call was erroneous and Hasselbeck's hit was legal. Regardless, the Seahawks lost the Super Bowl 21–10 to the Pittsburgh Steelers. The general feeling, however, was that the game was swayed by bad officiating. Sometime after, Holmgren publicly criticized the outcome of the game, saying that he didn't think his team would have to take on both the Steelers and the officials. Holmgren, amazingly, wasn't fined by the NFL for his comments, but the 12th man put out tip jars all over town to cover the charge, just in case.

Declining Decade

The Seahawks made a brief playoff appearance the next season but hit the skids afterward with two mediocre—at best—seasons. Holmgren eventually gave way to coach-in-waiting Jim Mora—a former Washington Husky—whose first, and, as it turns out, only season as coach in 2009 was a drab 5–11. Mora was fired just five days after the final game of the season. His one year at the helm was the shortest head-coaching stint in team history. Former University of Southern California coach Pete Carroll was named the team's new head coach just days later.

Chapter Three

Seattle's Stanley Cup Champions

The Triumph of the Metropolitans

Canada is the birthplace of hockey, and the Stanley Cup is the Holy Grail. But many years ago, when the Stanley Cup measured only a few inches tall, an American team from Seattle took home the title of the best team in North America. The team to own this glorious distinction was the 1917 Seattle Metropolitans of the Pacific Coast Hockey Association (PCHA).

In the early days of hockey when the Stanley Cup was still a challenge cup, the top team from the National Hockey Association (NHA) and the PCHA competed for the right to be named Cup champion. Today, the Stanley Cup is the property of the National Hockey League, and no other league can play for it. But in the early 20th century, almost any pro team could challenge the champions for Lord Stanley's Cup.

At the end of the 1917 season, the Montreal Canadiens won the NHA finals to earn the right to face off against the PCHA champion Seattle Metropolitans. The Canadiens traveled to Seattle to play the Metropolitans in a best-of-five series for the Stanley Cup. This was only the second time since the Cup was first awarded in 1883 that an American-based team had played for the championship. (The Portland Rosebuds, one year earlier, had lost the Cup to the Montreal Canadiens.)

The Canadiens had legendary players in their lineup in 1917, including forward Didier Pitre, goaltender Georges Vezina and natural goal-scorer Edouard "Newsy" Lalonde, but the Metropolitans were no pushovers, either. Seattle goaltender Harry "Hap" Holmes was a veteran of the professional hockey circuit and had played in the eastern leagues for many years before jumping to the PCHA, and center Bernie Morris led his team in scoring that year with 37 goals in 24 games. The series had all the makings for an exciting, high-scoring adventure.

The first game of the series on March 17, 1917, was held at the Seattle Ice Arena near the present-day Olympic Hotel. Led by Pitre, who scored four goals, the Canadiens walked away with an easy 8–4 victory. The early loss did not bring Seattle down. In the second game, the Metropolitans hammered the Canadiens 6–1 to tie up the series. The beating in Game 2 seemed to take all the energy out of the Montreal squad, and the Metropolitans walked away with two easy wins in Games 3 and 4 with scores of 4–1 and 9–1, respectively. Holmes was probably the most solid player on the Seattle team, finishing the series with a 2.90 goals-against average, and Morris got the job done in the other end of the rink, scoring 14 of Seattle's series 23 goals.

The Metropolitans disposed of the Canadiens in four games to become the first U.S.-based team to have their names engraved on the Stanley Cup. However, as an interesting side note, all the players on the Metropolitans, save for Everard Carpenter, were born in Canada.

Seattle Hit by Pandemic

In only its second year of operation in the 1918–19 season, the NHL faced a major roadblock to establishing itself in North America. When the Spanish influenza plague began to affect hockey players in the U.S. and Canada, attendance across the league started to drop significantly. Government banners warning people about the deadly virus and how to avoid contracting it were plastered in every city. The NHL suddenly faced a harsh economic reality. To close operations meant to risk folding the entire league, and to continue to hold games was to risk the health of the public and the league's players. In the end, the NHL and the team owners decided to take the risk, continue the season and simply hope for the best.

With only the revenue from the arenas of the Montreal Canadiens, Ottawa Senators and Toronto Maple Leafs coming in that season, the NHL couldn't afford to postpone play until the influenza pandemic ran its course. Such was the case for the PCHA as well. Surviving the wars years left many PCHA teams a little thin in the wallet so they continued their season despite the government warnings and risk to their players.

The Seattle Metropolitans finished out the remainder of the 1918–19 season in second place overall in the PCHA behind their cross-border rivals the Vancouver Millionaires. The two teams faced off in a two-game total-goals series for the PCHA championship and the right to move on to the Stanley Cup finals against the NHL championship team. Seattle came out the victor in the Millionaires series with a two-game total score of 7–5. Seattle had earned the right to again play in the Stanley Cup finals against the NHL champion Montreal Canadiens.

The Canadiens management had some reservations about making the long trip west to meet the Metropolitans—the train ride was seven days, after all—but of greater concern was influenza. The players were going to be confined together on the train, and if just one player caught the flu then it would put the entire team at risk. The concerns ended up being swept aside given the importance of the match and the much-needed revenues that were needed in the league's coffers.

Despite all the warnings and threats of disease, the series between the Metropolitans and Canadiens got underway on March 19, 1919, in Seattle. The two squads faced off against each other in alternating games played under both eastern- and western-league rules. The PCHA played the game with the old system of seven men on the ice (the seventh being the rover, a player with no set position) instead of the six-man NHL rule. And so, with seven men on the ice, the Metropolitans won their first game by the convincing score of 7–0. The Canadiens bounced back with a 4–2 victory in Game 2 under the eastern rules. When the Metropolitans won the third game, the series seemed destined to be decided by the rules of the game and not by the quality of its players. However, by Game 4, both teams had adjusted to playing under the different systems and they finished with a 0–0 tie. (In the early days of hockey, overtime was not used to decide the fate of a game.) In Game 5, Seattle took a 3–0 lead early in the game as the Canadiens looked tired and sluggish on the ice. The worst among the Canadiens was defenseman Joe Hall, who labored up and down the ice for the majority of the game. After two periods, Hall could barely stand on his skates and was forced to remove himself from the game because of dizziness and a fever. Newsy Lalonde came to the rescue of the Canadiens and scored two goals to lead his team to a 4–3 comeback victory and a second chance at taking the Cup in the final game slated for April 1, 1919.

Everything came to a grinding halt when several of the Canadiens players began to exhibit flu-like symptoms the day of Game 6 and were sent to hospital. It was confirmed later that they had contracted the dreaded Spanish influenza. The Metropolitans escaped unscathed, but five Montreal players had to remain in a Seattle hospital. All recovered, except for Joe Hall and manager George Kennedy who both later died from flu complications. Because of the numbers of players forced out of the lineup, the Canadiens had to forfeit the game and thus hand over the Stanley Cup to the Metropolitans. Seattle manager Pete Muldoon, however, refused to accept the Cup in forfeiture and preferred to have no champion that year. This was the first time in Stanley Cup history that no one was named the winner.

Chapter Four

Boom and Bust—the Seattle Supersonics

Gin and Sonic

In 1966, Boeing was awarded a government contract to build a supersonic transport plane to compete with the Concorde. In 1967, the new NBA team in Seattle used that top-of-mind local project as inspiration for its own name—the Supersonics. Alas, the contract was cancelled in 1971 and the Supersonic Transport (SST) was never built. With the loss of the SST contract and other government work, plus a downturn in the civilian aviation market, Boeing reduced its staff by some 60,000 workers, prompting a few local realtors to put up a billboard near the airport that read: "Will the last person leaving SEATTLE— turn out the lights."

Established in 1967, the Seattle Supersonics were the city's first major-league sports franchise. Over the next 40 NBA seasons, the Sonics made the playoffs 22 times, and in 1979, won the league championship, securing the win of the first modern-day professional sports championship trophy of any kind for Seattle.

The Sonics debuted on October 13, 1967, losing in an away game to the San Francisco Warriors. The first Sonics home game was played on October 20—another loss—this time to fellow expansion team, the San Diego Rockets. The first win for Seattle came the next day on the road against the Rockets. Ultimately, the Sonics won only 23 games that first year, but since they were an expansion team, who was counting?

Lenny Wilkens—Master Multi-tasker

Led by player/coach Lenny Wilkens and All-Star Spencer Haywood, the Supersonics enjoyed their first winning season in 1971–72, finishing with a record of 47–35. But then, to much fan objection, Wilkens was traded to the Cleveland Cavaliers at the end of the season. And in acquiring Haywood, the Sonics violated an NBA rule against signing players less than four years out of high school. At the time, Haywood had been out of school for only three years. Haywood and team owner Sam Schulman fought the league all the way to the Supreme Court, which ended up ruling against the league. The decision paved the way for what became the NBA's hardship rule. Under the new regulation, a college dropout or a player less than four years removed from high school who could demonstrate some level of financial, domestic or academic adversity could be signed by an NBA team as a hardship case. That rather shaky standard led to the removal of the rule in 1976.

A Celtic Comes to Town

Legendary Boston Celtic center Bill Russell joined the Sonics for the 1973–74 season as coach and general manager. In doing so, the 11-time NBA champion and NBA Hall of Famer became the league's highest paid executive at a reported $125,000 a year. By the end of his second full season, Russell had the Sonics in the playoffs for the first time in club history. They were eliminated in the second round by the Golden State Warriors, the eventual NBA champs that year.

After four years with the team, Russell left the Sonics because the players were having trouble grasping his defensive, team-oriented concept that so galvanized his championship Celtics teams. Russell was replaced by assistant coach Bob Hopkins, who happened to be his cousin. But Russell wasn't done with the Seattle limelight. In 1985, the Mercer Island, Washington, resident took one of only two parts in the Seattle Children's Theater production of *The Former One-on-One Champion*. Russell played an aging basketball player.

Out of the Ashes...

The 1977–78 season started out as nothing short of a disaster. After winning only five of their first 22 games, new Sonics coach Bob Hopkins was fired and replaced by former Sonics coach and player Lenny Wilkens. The team responded with a solid third-place finish and an unlikely run through the playoffs that brought them all the way to the NBA finals. Against the Washington Bullets, the Sonics actually held the series lead twice (at 2–1 and 3–2) before losing the finals to Washington in a dramatic Game 7 in Seattle.

Will this New Home be Big Enough for You?

Demand for Sonics tickets was so high in 1978 that the team moved to the Kingdome where they played their home games for the next seven seasons. In their original Seattle Center Coliseum home, the Sonics could only sell about 12,000 tickets (not that they always did, of course), but in the Kingdome, the team could double, and sometimes triple, that figure. In fact, once settled into the Kingdome, the Sonics shattered NBA attendance records. In 1978, there was a record crowd for a playoff game—39,457—and another record was set in 1980 with 40,172 fans in attendance. In the 1979–80 season, the Sonics averaged a record 21,725 fans per game. The big Kingdome basketball crowds of this era were inspired to go to games by some of the franchise's best teams ever, including the NBA championship team of 1979. And with the huge crowds came noise—lots of it. It didn't take long for the Kingdome to earn a reputation as the loudest arena in all of the NBA.

NBA Championship Year

As it turned out, the Sonics were so comfortable in their new Kingdome home that the team put together their best season to date in 1978–79, winning their first-ever division championship with a 52–30 record. In the playoffs, the Sonics blew past the L.A. Lakers and Phoenix Suns before meeting up with the Washington Bullets in the NBA finals. Playoff experience and a lineup packed with superstar talent—including Jack Sikma, Freddie Brown, Paul Silas, Marvin Webster, Gus "The Wizard" Williams and finals MVP Dennis Johnson—proved too much for the Bullets this time. The Supersonics beat the Washington Bullets in five games to claim Seattle's first-ever NBA crown.

It Takes a Village

During the Sonics' 40 years in Seattle, home court was played in five different buildings. For the Sonics' first 11 years in action, home games were played at the Seattle Center Coliseum. Then they were moved to the Kingdome to support rocketing fan interest. Occasionally during these years, the team also played home games at the Hec Edmundson Pavilion the UW campus. Such was the case in 1981 when the defending champions found the Kingdome unavailable for Game 5 of the Western Conference finals against the L.A. Lakers. In going from the Kingdome to Hec Ed for that game, the Sonics went from the largest venue in the NBA to one of the smallest—and lost.

In 1985, it was back to the Coliseum for the next nine regular seasons, and while the Coliseum was torn down and resurrected as Key Arena, the Sonics played their home games in the Tacoma Dome from 1994 to 1995. With Key Arena ready in 1995, the Sonics went back to Seattle, where games were easily accessible to fans once more.

Basketball Game Rained Out

After seven years playing in the Kingdome, the Sonics returned to the Seattle Center Coliseum for the 1985–86 season. On January 5, 1986, during a game against the Phoenix Suns, water from a downpour outside leaked through the aging Coliseum roof and onto the court forcing the first "rainout" in NBA history.

This Guy can Score from "Downtown"

The NBA introduced the three-point line in 1979, and sharp-shooting Sonic "Downtown" Freddie Brown became the league's first-ever percentage leader in three-point shooting (.443). By the time Brown finished his 13-year career, he scored more points than any player in Sonics history...that is, until Gary Payton came along. But Brown still holds the team record for most points in a regular season game with 58. The Sonics retired Brown's number 32 jersey in 1986. He later became a banking executive in Seattle after his retirement from the NBA.

Hey, Nice Trade...Not!

In what is considered one of the worst draft-day deals in NBA history, the Seattle Supersonics traded Scottie Pippen—the fifth pick in the 1987 draft—to the Chicago Bulls for center Olden Polynice. Pippin, of course, went on to win six NBA titles with Chicago. Polynice, on the other hand, didn't perform quite as admirably. Pulling the trigger on the deal was Supersonics general manager Bob Whitsitt, or as fans had dubbed him, "Trader Bob." Whitsitt soon made better trades, one day assembling a team that played in (but lost) the 1996 NBA championship.

Nice Bling

The only Seattle Supersonic to win an NBA Slam Dunk contest was Lonnie Shelton. So vicious were his thundering slams, he once bent the rim during a game and teams had to wait out a 30-minute delay while a new rim was installed. The excessive jam also cost Shelton a technical foul and a fine. He kept the rim as a keepsake, wearing it like a necklace in the locker room after the game.

Too Cool for School

At a height of six-foot-eleven and a jump-reach that put him in the clouds, Shawn Kemp was one of the most coveted high school basketball players in the country in 1988. But with academics keeping him ineligible, Kemp's college basketball career at the University of Kentucky never got off the ground. Kemp was eligible for the 1989 NBA draft, however, and the Seattle Supersonics didn't hesitate to pick up the supremely athletic 19-year-old, his age making him the youngest player in the NBA at the time. Kemp's NBA skills proved to be raw that first year, but the rookie still managed to make a name for himself—as the "Reign Man"—for his spectacular above-the-rim play and 70 blocked shots in only 81 games played. Kemp went on to play eight seasons for the Sonics, including the 1995–96 season in which the team set a franchise record with 64 wins and an appearance in the NBA finals.

Can You Say "Overconfident"?

Behind the skills of Gary Payton, Detlef Schrempf, Kendall Gill and Kemp, the Sonics played to an NBA-best 63–19 record in the 1993–94 season. The Sonics figured they'd make quick work of eighth-seeded Denver in the first round of the playoffs, but the Nuggets had other ideas and produced an overtime upset in Game 5. It was the first time in NBA playoff history that a number-one seed lost to a number-eight seed. Indeed, Sonics teams under coach George Karl in the 1990s gained something of a reputation for choking in the early playoff rounds. For example, the Sonics again made the playoffs the following season but were eliminated in the first round.

Coach Knows Iambic Pentameter

Among the Sonics' more colorful coaches was Karl, who was at the team's helm from 1991 to 1998. The winningest coach in team history, Karl's teams won 357 games during his seven-season run, second only to the Chicago Bulls during those same years. But along with the victories, fans loved Karl for his somewhat wrinkled look and fearless, outspoken style. He often butted heads with Sonics players and top brass. However, he showed a softer side on his weekly radio show, on which it wasn't surprising to hear Karl read a poem.

Payton Gets a Grip on Jordan

A perennial playoff team in the 1990s, the Sonics returned to the NBA finals in 1996. Seattle was up against a Michael Jordan–led Chicago Bulls team (that also included Scottie Pippin, remember him?). Chicago had dominated the NBA that year, going 72–10. The Bulls jumped out to a 3–0 series lead before the Sonics could even attempt to slow down the train. In Game 4, Gary "The Glove" Payton tightened his grip and applied some tenacious defense on Jordan and held the Bulls' superstar to a career NBA finals low of only 23 points. The Sonics went on to mount a valiant series comeback, winning Games 4 and 5, but ultimately dropping the finals in Game 6.

Takin' Out the Trash

"The Glove" Payton had a smothering style of defensive play and, along with these formidable defender skills, was the Sonics' all-time points leader. He was also notorious for something else. The Glove was one of the NBA's most prolific trash-talkers. His open-mouth policy led to many a technical foul—the third most in NBA history—and Payton often said his trash-talking style was simply a way to test the mental toughness of his opponents.

Mr. Sonic

Among the more beloved former Sonics is Nate McMillan. As a player, he spent his entire 12-year career with Seattle (1986–98). During his rookie year, McMillan once dished out 25 assists in a single game, an NBA record he still shares with Ernie DiGregorio. McMillan was a superb defensive player as well, and in the 1993–94 season led the league in steals per game. He also notched four triple-doubles in his career. McMillan is one of only four Sonics players to have their jersey numbers retired. He joined the ranks with Freddie Brown, Jack Sikma and Lenny Wilkens.

After his retirement in 1998, McMillan rejoined the team as an assistant coach, and then took over as head coach in 2000, making him the youngest head coach in the NBA at 36 years old. During the 2004–05 season, he directed the Sonics to 52 wins and a Northwest Division title before elimination in the Conference semifinals.

In a strange turn of off-season events that had Sonics fans scratching their heads, McMillan didn't reach agreeable terms on a new contract with the team. By the beginning of the next season, McMillan was head coach of the rival Portland Trailblazers. The move was puzzling, but McMillan is still welcome around town, and after 19 years as a player and coach in Seattle, a seat will always be available for the man who was known as "Mr. Sonic."

What's in a Name?

Can you attach real names to the three former Sonics who earned these nicknames: 3D, X-Man and Big Smooth? If you answered Dale Ellis, Xavier McDaniel and Sam Perkins, give yourself a fist-bump.

Most Popular Benchwarmer

Center-forward Steve Scheffler was a perennial benchwarmer for the Seattle Supersonics from 1992 to 1997. Nevertheless, he became a fan favorite for his towel-wavin', high-fivin' sideline enthusiasm. When the Sonics had a game well in hand (or well out of hand), Scheffler often entered the lineup to a loud ovation. Fans couldn't wait for Scheffler to score so they could lend him a cheer.

Ownership Trail Heads out of Town

The Sonics were founded under the ownership of Los Angeles businessman Sam Schulman who, with business partner, Eugene Klein, paid

$1.8 million to the NBA for the team's expansion rights. In 1983, outdoor billboard king Barry Ackerley took ownership, paying Schulman and Klein $13 million for the team. In 2001, Ackerley turned the team over to a local ownership group led by Starbucks Coffee CEO Howard Schultz. Price tag: $200 million. Schultz's group only lasted a few years and sold the team for $350 million in 2006 to an Oklahoma ownership group led by Clay Bennett. At one time, Bennett was part owner of the San Antonio Spurs and facilitated the deal that brought the New Orleans Hornets to Oklahoma City when the team was temporarily displaced by Hurricane Katrina. Bennett's group even tried to purchase control of the Hornets, but that offer was rebuffed by owner George Shinn.

Upon purchase of the Supersonics, however, Bennett stated he would make a "good faith" effort to keep the team in Seattle, despite what he and the NBA called an inadequate arena. Only 12 years earlier, the Seattle Center Coliseum had been renovated and renamed the Key Arena. Following that 1994 $100-million upgrade, NBA commissioner David Stern called the Sonics' new digs a "beautiful building" and one the people of Seattle should be proud of. By 2006, Stern's attitude about Key Arena flipped to an entirely negative assessment as he and Bennett set in motion what many fans suspected was an agenda to move the team to Oklahoma City. Confirmation of that suspicion came from the unlikely source of Aubrey McClendon, an Oklahoma businessman and a minority partner in the new ownership group. McClendon was quoted in an Oklahoma City newspaper, the *Journal Record*, as saying, "We didn't buy the team to keep it in Seattle, we hoped to come here." That slip of the tongue cost McClendon $250,000. Make that check out to the NBA, please.

Purging the team of its two best players, superstars Ray Allen and Rashard Lewis, the Sonics finished their 2007–08 season—their last in Seattle—an abysmal 20–62, the worst playing record in the team's history. Meanwhile, after a series of lawsuits and protracted court litigation, the City of Seattle eventually settled with the new Sonics owners on the remaining years of the lease at Key Arena. Following that, the owners wasted no time in loading up the moving vans and shipping the team off to Oklahoma City where they're now known as the Thunder. As a small and fairly inconsequential consolation, among the rubble of the settlement is an agreement that allows Seattle to keep the Supersonics name, team colors and team history. Thanks, that makes it all better!

Former Sonics Freddie Brown and Gary Payton are active in early efforts to establish a new NBA team in Seattle. Payton has even gone so far as to state that he does not want his jersey number retired in Oklahoma City, should that day ever come.

Adopt-a-Blazer

When you mix Portland Trailblazers coach and Mr. Sonic Nate McMillan with starting Blazers guard (and former Husky) Brandon Roy, then add a dash of Seattle Prep phenom Martell Webster, what do you get? A lot of Portland Trailblazers fans—in Seattle. Such a large fan interest in the former "I-5" NBA rival was unfathomable a few years ago, but given the departure (or theft, to many fans) of the Sonics to Oklahoma City, and the Seattle-like flavor of the Blazers lineup, many die-hard NBA fans around the Puget Sound adopted the Portland Trailblazers as their new favorite team. In the absence of a true home team, it'll just have to do.

Indeed, one of the hot rumors during the early stages of the Sonics "heist" was that Portland Trailblazers owner Paul Allen (who also owns the Seattle Seahawks of the NFL) was going to move his Trailblazers team to Seattle if the Oklahoma City move by the Sonics was successful, and only if he was not able to get a new deal completed in Portland to continue playing at the Rose Garden. But Allen got the deal he wanted in Portland, and the rumor died a quiet death. For Portland fans, 'twas a good death; for Seattle Sonics fans, it was another bizarre twist that only fueled the frustration of the day.

Sonics Retire Jerseys and a Microphone

In total, the Seattle Supersonics retired six jersey numbers and a microphone in the team's 40 seasons. The jersey numbers retired were Gus Williams' number 1, Nate McMillan's number 10, Lenny Wilkens' number 19, Spencer Haywood's number 24, Freddie Brown's number 32 and Jack Sikma's number 43. In 1992, in honor of departing play-by-play announcer Bob Blackburn and his 25 years as the voice of the Sonics, the team symbolically retired his microphone. The merriment was tainted, though, because Blackburn called his retirement "forced" as the team began to envision his younger play-by-play partner, Kevin Calabro, as the team's future signature voice. Calabro remained the team "voice" until the end of its run in Seattle, and then decided against staying with the Sonics/Thunder through the team's move to Oklahoma City. Take that, Thunder!

Squatch Goes Home

What can you say about Squatch? The surprisingly athletic and self-assured forest creature came out of the woods to become the Sonics' mascot in the late 1990s and quickly became a fan favorite for his high-flying slams and court-side pranks. Squatch—full name, Sasquatch—lost his gig when the Sonics left town. He was turned down for unemployment insurance when he listed his address as "the woods." Heartbroken at the team's departure, he was last seen with a Sonics jersey over his shoulder, lumbering back into his deep-forest home somewhere near the Canadian border. Long live Squatch!

Storm Still Brewing

Although the Sonics disappeared into the Midwest, professional basketball in Washington didn't go away altogether. No, sir. The Women's National Basketball Association's (WNBA) Seattle Storm, once part of the Supersonics empire, was allowed to break free from the Oklahoma-bound mother ship and stay home in the friendly confines of Key Arena—and Seattle is glad to have them. The now locally owned franchise stages a family-friendly show with an all-kid dance squad, a mascot named Doppler and a theme song called "Thunderstruck" (by AC/DC). The Storm knows how to win, too. A consistent playoff contender, the team brought home a WNBA championship in 2004—only the second major professional sports championship trophy the city of Seattle has ever seen (the Sonics brought home the first one, some 25 years earlier). In 2004, Anne Donovan also took home the honor of being the first female coach to win a WNBA championship. In addition, the Seattle Storm still boasts two of the best female basketball players in the world in All-Stars Lauren Jackson and Sue Bird. A member of the WNBA All-Decade team, Jackson is the youngest and fastest WNBA player to score 4000 career points. Bird, on the other hand, has the distinction of being one of only seven women to win an NCAA championship (with Connecticut), to capture an Olympic gold medal (with the U.S. team in Athens 2004) and to also win a WNBA championship (with the Storm). You go, girls!

Like many WNBA players, Jackson and Bird take their skills overseas during the off-season, playing for professional teams in Russia, South Korea and Australia, Jackson's home country.

Chapter Five

Thunderboats Rule the Waters

In 2009, the American Power Boat Association (APBA) held only eight hydroplane-boat races, and two of them took place in the state of Washington. Such is the popularity of power-boat racing in the state. Few places in America hold the noisy "Hydros" (aka Thunderboats) in such esteem, and few states display their fan support like Washington, with fans showing up on the shores of Lake Washington (Seattle) and the Columbia River (Tri-Cities) by the hundreds of thousands. The fervor for these races is so great that the Tri-Cities Water Follies are traditionally held the weekend before the Seafair hydro races in Seattle so as to cut down on the teams' travel expenses. In the Tri-Cities races, the unlimited hydroplanes compete for The Columbia Cup on a course said to be among the fastest on the circuit.

Not a lot of people in America enjoy the legacy of this sport like Washingtonians do. And that passion goes way back—some 60 years.

Record Speed in Slow Motion

The first Seafair boat race was run on Seattle's Green Lake in 1950. This was also the inaugural year of Seafair itself—the city's attempt to establish an annual community festival. This first-year festival included a parade along with various athletic and community events. It was something of a shakedown cruise for the larger Seafair festival the following year that celebrated Seattle's centennial. For this, festival designers wanted to go big—not only to honor the city's first 100 years but also as a way to attract some national press. At the time, Seattle didn't have any pro sports franchises, but the city had a strong desire to play host to one.

Meanwhile, on June 27, 1950, Stanley Sayres was taking his boat, *Slo-mo-shun*, for its own shakedown cruise off the shores of Lake Washington. But there was nothing "slo" about his unlimited hydroplane as he pushed it to a world record speed of 160.32 miles per hour over a mile-long straightaway. Sayres captured more than a world record; he also captured the imagination, hopes and dreams of local sports fans hungry for major-league success of any kind. And he made good. Piloted by Ted Jones, *Slo-mo-shun* easily won the APBA Gold Cup—boat racing's biggest prize—in Detroit in 1950. By virtue of that win, Seattle hosted the Gold Cup competition the next year on Lake Washington. Sayres successfully defended his title in 1951, as well as for the next three years—keeping the competition on Lake Washington during each of those seasons. In the *Slo-mo-shun IV* and *Slo-mo-shun V*, Sayres anchored his legacy as the first "major league" sports "franchise owner" in Seattle and solidified the region's self-proclaimed title as the "Boating Capital of the World." The Stan Sayres Pits on Lake Washington, where the hydroplane races are based every summer, are named in his honor.

Hydros Owned this State

Until the Seattle Supersonics came along in 1967, the unlimited hydro races enjoyed a measure of exclusivity as the only "game" in town (of a professional sort, anyway). To be sure, the "Thunderboats" ruled the Puget Sound sports kingdom in the 1960s. It wasn't uncommon for as many as three local TV stations to offer live coverage of the races, along with a dozen or more radio stations.

With national attention already on Seattle during the 1962 World's Fair, Seafair and the unlimited hydroplane races experienced unprecedented publicity. And in the late 1950s to early 1960s, the sport had a legitimate superstar in Bill Muncey who piloted the Seattle-based *Miss Thriftway* (renamed *Miss Century 21* in 1962 in honor of the World's Fair) to four APBA Gold Cups and three national championships. Muncey, aboard various boats throughout his career, eventually won eight Gold Cups and seven national championships, becoming the sport's winningest driver with a seemingly untouchable 62 career victories. Driving his own *Miss Atlas Van Lines* in 1981, Muncey died at age 52 in a "blowover" accident during a race in Acapulco, Mexico, in which the bow of his boat rose too high, allowing the wind to catch and flip the boat upside down.

Along Comes Chip

Tragic as the accident was, the open driver position aboard the *Miss Atlas Van Lines* was nothing short of a plum opportunity for whoever took the helm. Hand-picked by Fran Muncey (Bill's wife), that enviable job went to a Newport High School (Bellevue) and Washington State University graduate with an education degree (cum laude, class of 1976): Chip Hanauer. Hanauer bought his first racing boat at age nine with money earned from a paper route, and with only one victory under his belt as an adult, landing a ride aboard the *Miss Atlas Van Lines* was a huge break.

Hanauer's replacement of Muncey wasn't the first time the young boater was called on to take the seat of a driver killed in a racing accident. In 1977, Jerry Bangs lost his life in a heat race on Lake Washington and Hanauer was recruited to take his place. And then later, with the Fran Muncey team, Hanauer had a boat and a team that were every bit as good as his skills. He was off and running through a career that nearly eclipsed the racing icon he replaced. Aboard the *Miss Atlas Van Lines*, *Miller American*, *Atlas/Miller* and *Circus Circus* (all Fran Muncey–owned boats), Hanauer won seven Gold Cups. By the end of his career, highlighted by a long run (1992–99) aboard the fast and famous *Miss Budweiser*, Hanauer won a record total of 11 Gold Cups and amassed 61 career victories, one short of Muncey's career total. Budweiser teams, led by legendary team owner Bernie Little, were notoriously well funded, and with Hanauer at the helm, they ruled the unlimited courses through much of the 1990s.

During his highly successful racing career, Hanauer helped usher in major innovations that transformed his sport. First, in the mid-1980s, turbine helicopter engines replaced piston power plants, and faster, more dangerous speeds soon followed. At about the same time as turbine helicopter engines came into the picture, enclosed canopies were installed on unlimited boats, greatly increasing driver safety in the new age of speedy turbine engines. Ever mindful of driver safety, Hanauer was instrumental in the development of the canopies and the effort to make them mandatory.

But the safety canopies couldn't save Hanauer (or other boaters) from harm altogether. His high-risk career led to a myriad of injuries including fractured vertebrae, concussions, broken ribs, neck pain and a baffling neurological disorder that cost Hanauer his voice. Beginning in 1992 and for the next three years, he could barely muster a strained whisper, and the best cause doctors could come up with was stress.

Hanauer called that period the darkest of his life. In 1996 a conclusive diagnosis was reached: spasmodic dysphonia, or SD. The treatment was Botox. Hanauer was treated by specialists in New York and at the UW Medical Center in Seattle, and he got his voice back. Hanauer continues with treatment and speech therapy to this day.

After Hanauer's final retirement in 1999 (he tried and failed at retiring a few times), he dusted off his education degree and returned to the classroom to teach kids with behavior disorders.

The Milkman on a Beer Boat

The *Miss Budweiser*, under the ownership and leadership of Bernie Little, was arguably the most dominating boat in all of hydroplane racing history. The first driver to win a race aboard the *Miss Budweiser* was Bill Brow, a Burien, Washington, resident and local dairyman. In 1965 in Seattle, Brow set an APBA qualifying record of better than 120 miles per hour aboard the *Miss Exide* (which later became the *Miss Budweiser* with Little's acquisition), and he was dubbed "The World's Fastest Milkman." Brow captured the *Miss Budweiser*'s first-ever racing trophy during the inaugural unlimited hydro race in the Tri-Cities. Held on July 25, 1966, the event was then called the Atomic Cup Regatta and Little's *Miss Budweiser*, with Brow at the wheel, swept each of the heats to capture top honors.

After his first win in the Tri-Cities race, Little and the *Miss Budweiser* went on to notch a record 134 victories and 14 APBA Gold Cups. Indeed, the *Miss Budweiser* represented not only the "King of Beers," but was also the king of boat racing.

Who Is William Rhodes Jr.?

You might know him as Bill O'Mara, but he was actually born William Rhodes Jr. O'Mara. A sports broadcaster in western Washington for six decades, he was the hydros announcer, and, from 1951 to 1959, anchored the live hydroplane race broadcasts on KING TV. Early in his broadcast career in Seattle, however, O'Mara was asked to change his name from the aforementioned William Rhodes Jr. so as not to ruffle the feathers of one of the station's large advertisers, The Bon Marche, whose chief competition was a department store named Rhodes.

The Seafair race in 1951, covered by O'Mara, was the first live TV coverage of an unlimited race west of the Mississippi, and it was during that race that O'Mara became forever linked to one of the most famous moments in Seattle television. In the final heat of the day, the *Quicksilver*—a boat out of Portland, Oregon—crashed. Driver Orth Mathiot and on-board mechanic Thom Whittaker were both killed. Shaken and trembling, O'Mara proceeded to face the camera and recite *The Lord's Prayer*. Though O'Mara felt it was the right thing to do at the moment, he also wondered whether the act would ruin his career. On the contrary, O'Mara's compassionate recitation endeared him to legions of equally shaken TV viewers. Race fans were forever touched by the profound and historic moment.

Never one to be at a loss for words, O'Mara was still calling the play-by-play of high school sports in Anacortes, Washington, when he was

90 years old. He was thought to be the oldest working sportscaster in the nation. O'Mara passed away in 2009 at the age of 92.

Hello, This Is Pat O'Day

The other signature voice of Seafair hydroplane races is Pat O'Day. The legendary Seattle DJ has broadcast Seafair races on radio and TV since 1967. O'Day's co-host for his first Seafair broadcast in 1967 was singer Wayne Newton—he was in town for a concert at the Seattle Center Coliseum, and O'Day called on him as a favor for playing the singer's records.

The Flying Czech Meets Miss Wahoo

Before unlimited hydroplane driver Mira Slovak was racing away from the competition, he was racing away from Communists. In 1954, at the controls of a huge transport aircraft in Soviet airspace, the Czechoslovakia Airlines pilot overpowered an uncooperative co-pilot and pushed the airplane straight toward the ground, leveling out just in time to avoid crashing. Slovak, with a payload of fellow Czech defectors, flew his plane under the radar until safely through the Iron Curtain and in the friendlier skies of Frankfurt, West Germany. Slovak's freedom flight made him an instant worldwide celebrity.

Eventually making his way to the U.S., Slovak couldn't translate his popularity into work as a pilot until President Dwight D. Eisenhower signed an executive order that allowed the non-citizen to gain the radio operator's license he needed to fly. Then, while working as a crop-duster pilot in Yakima, Washington, Slovak was invited by real-estate developer Bill Boeing Jr., son of Boeing Company founder, William Boeing, to become Junior's personal pilot. Slovak accepted.

While in a Boeing hangar one day, Slovak caught a glimpse of a strange-looking boat under construction. It was the *Miss Wahoo*, named after Mrs. Boeing Jr.'s hometown in Nebraska. One thing led to another, and suddenly Slovak was asked to drive the boat. Not having floated on the water in anything faster than a rowboat, Slovak was hesitant at first but agreed. Under the tutelage of veteran driver Ted Jones, Slovak raced to a second-place finish in his first heat race at the 1956 Seafair. The next year, Slovak pushed the *Miss Wahoo* to victory at Lake Tahoe. And in winning the President's Cup aboard the *Miss Wahoo* on Lake Mead in 1959, Slovak was able to personally thank President Eisenhower for his executive order a few years earlier that allowed the former Czech to work as a pilot in the U.S.

By Air and Water

Slovak often had double-duty on race days: he piloted his race boat on the water and flew his stunt plane between heats. He won't openly admit to it now, but during performances in the Tri-Cities, he was known to have twice flown his stunt plane under the giant Blue Bridge that spans the Columbia River. "The Flying Czech"—as Slovak was known—hung up his life vest following the 1966 Seafair races in Seattle but continued flying in air races and as a captain for Continental Airlines.

The Hydroplane Hall of Champions

In 2009, Chip Hanauer and Bill Muncey were the first to be inducted into the Hydroplane and Race Boat Museum's Hall of Champions. The Kent, Washington-based museum opened in 1983 and is the only public museum dedicated exclusively to power-boat racing. Some of the sport's most famous boats have been restored by the museum and are on display, including the *Miss Wahoo*, *Slo-mo-shun* (*IV* and *V*), *Miss Thriftway* and the legendary *Miss Bardahl*, affectionately called the "Green Dragon."

Back on Green Lake

After 20-some years on Lake Washington, the hydroplanes returned to Seattle's Green Lake for races in 1975 and 1976. In those years, the limited inboards, or "flatbottoms" as they were known, competed for the Heidelberg Inboard World Championships. With boats reaching speeds up to 100 miles per hour, Green Lake became known as the fastest inboard racing course in the world.

Chapter Six

Sounders Kick It Up a Notch

The Feel-good Story of the Year

The Seattle Sounders Football Club (FC) team was hot before it even played its first game in 2009, selling 22,000 season tickets, a league record. The strong support for the new Major League Soccer (MLS) team was no surprise to front office and league officials who had long known of the region's high interest in the sport. But there was another unanticipated force at work: the departure of the Seattle Supersonics. A city that felt ditched by the unthinkable exit of an iconic sports franchise needed some love and got it with the well-timed arrival of the Sounders FC. Group hug, everybody.

With the new season up and running, the Sounders became the first MLS expansion team to win their first three games. And it was no fluke. Team success continued throughout the year, first with the win of the U.S. Open Cup, and then with a berth in the MLS playoffs—only the second time in league history that an expansion team made the playoffs in their first year. In Seattle, the Sounders played the Houston Dynamo to a 0–0 draw in the first game of a two-game aggregate series (meaning the team with the most combined points after two games, wins). In Houston for Game 2, the Sounders forced overtime before dropping the match, and the series, 1–0.

The Hollywood Connection

The Sounders FC ownership group includes a Hollywood insider, a Hollywood star and a guy who could buy Hollywood. Joe Roth is a former chairman of both Walt Disney Studios and 20th Century Fox; comedian and actor Drew Carey is the current host of the popular game show *The Price is Right*; and Paul Allen is the co-founder of Microsoft and current owner of both the Portland Trailblazers and Seattle Seahawks. Team GM Adrian Hanauer, who was the United Soccer League (USL) Sounders' general manager and majority owner, has a stake in the Sounders FC as well.

International Star Power

Rosters on expansion teams in professional sports are typically filled with players lacking, shall we say, star power. The Sounders, however, not only landed a few of the hottest names in professional and international soccer, such as Freddie Ljungberg and Kasey Keller, but they also managed to attract one of the hottest names in coaching. Sigi Schmid is the most successful active coach in MLS history and has two MLS Cup championships to his credit. He is also widely acknowledged as one of the best college soccer coaches of all time after a 19-year stint at UCLA where he won three NCAA national championships—the first at the Kingdome in Seattle in 1985.

A Fashion Statement

Seattle Sounders FC midfielder Freddie Ljungberg is perhaps as famous for modeling underwear for Calvin Klein as he is for his work on the soccer field. Winner of numerous European championships and trophies, and a player in two World Cups, the native Swede joined an elite list, in 2003, of celebrities parading around in Calvin Klein garb: singer/actor Mark Wahlberg, former Oregon Duck and Olympic pole vaulter Tom Hintnaus and actress Brooke Shields. Ljungberg was also voted Sweden's best dressed man in 2002.

Mr. Magoo Tends Goal

Signing Kasey Keller, a local boy who made good on the soccer field, was a coup for the

Sounders. The pride of Lacey's North Thurston High School, Keller was a first-team All-American soccer player for the University of Portland in 1991. He spent some time playing for the Portland Timbers of the Western Soccer Alliance and the U.S. National team before moving on and taking his game to the international level. Keller tended goal for teams in England, Spain and Germany, while also helping various U.S. clubs challenge for the FIFA World Cup. In England, Millwall fans called Keller "Mr. Magoo" upon learning he wears contact lenses (which makes you wonder if the British are all that familiar with Mr. Magoo…). Considered one of the best goalkeepers to play the game, Keller is also a three-time Soccer Athlete of the Year winner.

Walk This Way

Sounders midfielder Osvaldo "Ozzie" Alonso is a Cuban defector. As a member of the Cuban national team in 2007, Alonso simply walked away from the squad during a shopping trip to a Wal-Mart store in Houston, Texas. The Cuban team lost another player, Lester Moré, to defection later that same trip.

Husky Makes the Team

One of the Sounders' other goalkeepers, Chris Eylander, is a local boy—a product of Auburn

Riverside High School and the University of Washington. He started every game (39) in his final two seasons as a UW Husky.

Fans Have a Voice, and Vote

Minority owner Drew Carey promised to give season-ticket holders more than a seat at Qwest Field, the Sounders' home pitch—these special fans also got a say in team matters. In one of the more unique fan/team relationships in professional sports (at least, in the U.S.), Sounders FC season-ticket holders are members of the Alliance in which they can vote on any number of team issues, including whether to fire the general manager. The idea was Carey's, who was inspired by similar relationships between fans and soccer teams in Europe. Carey is the Alliance chairman and hosts annual meetings.

The Name Lives On

It was also Carey's idea to submit the team name to a fan vote. But on the original ballot, the option "Sounders" was not among the choices. Fans made it clear that the local iconic soccer name should be considered, so team officials (Carey among them) agreed to add a space on the ballot for a write-in suggestion. "Sounders," or some variation of the name, was the runaway winner, beating out Seattle Alliance, Seattle Republic and Seattle FC. "Sounders" was first used in 1973 and also came about by fan vote. In fact, the new Seattle MLS team is the third locally based soccer club to use the Sounders name. First there was the North American Soccer League team that folded with the league in 1983, and then there was the United Soccer League Sounders that essentially disbanded as part of the agreement to establish an MLS team in Seattle. The official team name stands as the Seattle Sounders FC.

Making Waves

Carey wasn't done with his bright ideas. A soccer team in a region with a strong musical heritage (from Jimi Hendrix to Pearl Jam) should have a marching band, or so Carey thought. Thus, the Sound Wave was created. The 53-piece band marches in from Pioneer Square before each MLS game and sets the vibe for every Sounders FC match at Qwest Field.

The Cup Stops Here

For a little icing on a successful first-season cake, the MLS awarded the location of the 2009 MLS Cup to Seattle. The league's premier event was played on November 22, and Real Salt Lake won over the favored L.A. Galaxy team that had David Beckham on its roster.

Chapter Seven

Campus Classics—From the Champs to the Chumps

College Football—Throwing Around the Pigskin

In the Beginning

The University of Washington played its first football game on Thanksgiving Day, November 28, 1889. Only a few of the UW players had ever played football before, and their opponents were a group of "veteran" players from a variety of eastern U.S. schools who had formed a club team for the sport of it. UW lost 20–0 on a field that measured 110 yards—the standard size in the 19th century.

Road Trip Number One

UW's first game out of state was against Oregon Agricultural College (which is known today as Oregon State University) on December 4, 1897. Playing a tough three-game season, UW lost to the Oregon school 16–0 but did manage to beat the Seattle YMCA club earlier that year, 10–0. The other game came against the Seattle Athletic Club, a 10–6 loss.

Rivalry Number One

The first cross-state rivalry game between UW and Washington State University was played to a tie in 1900 when WSU was known as Washington Agricultural College. Today, the Huskies hold an overall advantage, 65–31–6.

Celeb Number One

In what might have been the first football game attended by a famous celebrity, UW hosted the University of Nevada in Seattle in 1903 and played under the watchful eye of Nez Perce Chief Joseph. Through an interpreter (UW professor Edmond B. Meany, the chief's friend and host, whom Joseph named "Three-Knives"), the famous Nez Perce leader told Meany he "saw a lot of white men almost fight today," and that "I do not think this good." But Joseph went on to say he was pleased that Washington won the game. Final score: 2–0.

Record Streak

From the end of the 1907 season to the second game of 1917, the University of Washington never lost a game—a stretch that included 59 victories

and four tie-games. The 63-game unbeaten streak
is a college football record that stands today. During
that incredible run, legendary coach Gil Dobie
(1908–16) led his teams to 39 consecutive wins,
a record that stood some 40 years until it was
broken by the University of Oklahoma. UW
offensive units were unstoppable in nine seasons
under the cigar-smoking hall-of-fame coach,
and the defenses were equally tough. Opponents
rarely scored in an era when the same 11 men
played both offense and defense.

No Bowling

Despite the record run of UW victories and
seasons, Dobie-coached teams never played in
a bowl game. As a matter of fact, the Rose Bowl
was just about the *only* bowl game in those days,
and from 1903 to 1915, no Rose Bowl games
were played at all. The story goes that in the
1902 Rose Bowl—the first-ever post-season bowl
game—Stanford was getting waxed by the University of Michigan so badly that the California
team gave up in the third quarter. Disheartened
by the lopsided game (49–0), the Tournament of
Roses Committee thought things might turn out
better with polo. When that sport drew only
a small crowd in 1903, the committee ran chariot
races (no kidding) for a few years as an alternative.
In 1916, the Rose Bowl game was reinstated

(though the game wasn't actually called the "Rose Bowl" until 1923).

At the end of the 1915 season, WSU and UW were both undefeated, but the WSU Cougars won the Rose Bowl invitation after an analysis of comparative scores. The team went on to beat Brown, 14–0, in the New Year's Day game of 1916. The next season, Dobie's last in Seattle, the Huskies were again unbeaten but lost a Rose Bowl berth, this time to Oregon, also an undefeated team. Earlier that year, the budding rivals had played to a scoreless tie in their game against each other. So what was the compelling and deciding factor for the Rose Bowl committee as to where to hold the game? Train fare. Seems Eugene to Pasadena was much cheaper than from Seattle.

Message from Above

During a 1915 Huskies game against the University of California, an ambitious pilot flew his new-fangled "hydroaeroplane" low over the playing field of the UW campus. Fans at the game were "bombed" by a message written on pieces of cardboard that promoted the use of aircraft to protect the home front during wartime. Who was that pilot? William Boeing, founder of the Boeing Aircraft Company.

Players Go on Strike

Unfortunately, the Gil Dobie era ended on a rather sour note. In 1916, a two-day players' strike caught Dobie in a pickle—did he support the striking players who were protesting the suspension of a fellow player, or did he support the UW faculty who issued the suspension? Dobie sided with the players. Even though the strike was short and the season finished without a loss, the faculty decided not to renew Dobie's contract, citing a failure to perform his duties to build character on the field. Dobie continued his hall-of-fame career at the Naval Academy, Cornell University and Boston College before retiring in 1938 as one of the greatest college football coaches of all time. While at Cornell, Dobie coached another string of undefeated seasons, in 1921, 1922 and 1923. In his career, Dobie amassed 14 undefeated seasons.

No Squinting at Husky Stadium

The University of Washington lost nine games in the four years following Dobie's departure, which was enough to have fans screaming for changes. So, they got a new stadium that opened in 1920 with an original seating capacity of 30,000. The University of Washington stadium featured a dirt field and was specifically oriented at 18.167° south of due east to help minimize the glare from nearby Lake Washington. Construction was completed just 12 hours before kickoff of the first football game. The day before this game, a biplane taking aerial pictures of the new stadium, and with the words "Welcome Dartmouth" painted on the underside of its lower wings, crash-landed next to the stadium. Nobody was hurt, but UW lost the stadium opener to the East Coast school, 28–7. Today, thanks to numerous expansions throughout its long history, Husky Stadium now boasts a capacity of 72,500, making it the largest stadium in the Pacific Northwest.

The Sun Dodgers?

In 1922, the Huskies/Husky was the team name and mascot officially adopted by the University of Washington, beating out the one other finalist, the Malamutes. For a few years before that, however, UW athletic teams were known as the Sun Dodgers—a name taken from a banned campus magazine. Athletic officials didn't particularly care for the rather unappealing reference to cloudy Northwest weather (much less a mascot running around named Sunny the Sun Dodger), so they changed the team name to the Vikings during the Christmas break of 1921. That handle was quickly tossed by protesting students returning to campus. Going back to the drawing board came up with the Olympics, Northmen, Tyees,

Wolves, Malamutes and Huskies. At halftime of a basketball game against WSU on February 3, 1922, the Husky was announced as the new and official mascot of the University of Washington. There was no objection. The Sun Dodgers name lives on today as the name of UW's ultimate Frisbee team.

Harding's Last Stand

In the summer of 1923, Warren G. Harding was the first U.S. president to visit Alaska (though it was not state at the time). On his return trip, Harding stopped in Seattle on July 27 to give a speech to a large crowd at Husky Stadium. It was the last speech from the 29th president. Harding fell ill during the West Coast leg of his train trip and died a few days later—on August 2—in San Francisco.

A One-man Football Team

The stadium was broken in, new coach Enoch "Baggy" Bagshaw (himself a former UW player and credited with completing the school's first forward pass in 1906) was at the helm and a talented new player from Everett High School— George Wilson—was on the team. Wilson's football career in high school was the stuff of legends. His Everett High School teams (also coached by Bagshaw) were recognized as national champions after a 16–7 victory over a team from Cleveland, Ohio. Ahead of that game, the Everett Seagulls beat a team from The Dalles, Oregon (Oregon's best high school football team at the time), 90–7, and the University of Washington freshman team, 20–6.

The University of Washington squad of 1923 went 10–1–1. Halfback Wilson led a powerful offense through a thrilling season that included a number of notable firsts. This was the first-ever game against USC, won by the Huskies, 22–0. It was also the first sellout at the new Husky Stadium. The USC game heard the first-ever radio broadcast of a Huskies game, and last but certainly not least, this season provided the first-ever Huskies trip to the Rose Bowl where they played the Naval Academy to a 14–14 tie.

Wilson eventually gave Washington a couple more firsts. In 1925, he debuted as the school's consensus first-team All-American (as a halfback along with Red Grange of the University of Illinois) and led his team to a second Rose Bowl appearance. Then in 1951, Wilson was the first Husky to be elected into the College Football Hall of Fame.

UW entered the 1926 Rose Bowl game ranked third and with an offense that was leading the nation in scoring (for the second year in a row). Carrying the ball on almost every offensive play,

Wilson and his team were ahead of the University of Alabama in the second quarter when the Huskies star was knocked out cold and carried off the field. With Wilson out of the game, the Crimson Tide came storming back in the second half to take the lead. Washington's offense was dead in the water with Wilson out, and Alabama knew it (Wilson also played linebacker, so his injury was a double-whammy for the Huskies). But wait! What's this? *Wilson is coming back into the game?* Sure enough, Wilson woke up, shook the cobwebs off and stepped back on the field to bring the Huskies to within one point of Alabama late in the fourth quarter. But he threw an interception on UW's last drive of the game and Alabama held on. Final score: 20–19. Named the game's MVP (along with Alabama's Johnny Mack Brown), it was yet another thrilling performance by arguably the greatest Huskies football player of all time.

With his high school and college days behind him, Wilson tried pro football for a short while. The budding league struggled, though, and so did Wilson—his career as a football player ended in 1928.

Wilson also tried professional wrestling in Australia, but Australian law prohibited him from taking his earnings back to the United States so he returned to his homeland broke. He eventually settled into a career as a longshore-man in San Francisco and Everett before his death in 1963.

Before he died, however, there was one last proud moment for Wilson. In 1960, Jim Owens' Washington Huskies returned to the Rose Bowl and beat the University of Wisconsin 44–8 in the first-ever Rose Bowl victory for the school. Wilson was invited into the locker room for the post-game celebration where he was recognized and remem-bered fondly by many of the players and coaches. The aging Wilson said he was thrilled to not be forgotten.

Babe Makes Cougars Growl

Beginning in 1926, the Huskies' rival WSU Cougars began a 17-year span through what is arguably the greatest era in WSU football. Led by legendary coach Orin E. "Babe" Hollingbery, the Cougars won 93 games, lost 53, tied 14 and didn't lose a home game from 1926 to 1935. In 1930, Hollingbery led his team to a perfect 9–0 regular season record and a berth in the Rose Bowl. The Cougars lost that game 24–0 to Alabama.

The Cougars didn't gain another Rose Bowl invitation for 67 years—not until the Mike Price era. In the 14 years from 1989 to 2002, Price went 83–78, and, behind the strong arm of Ryan Leaf, took on an undefeated University of Michigan team in the 1998 Rose Bowl. The Cougars played well and led early in the game but lost 21–16 to the eventual co-national champion Wolverines.

The Big Train

It took six years for Husky Arnie Weinmeister to use up his college football eligibility. After playing in the 1942 season, he spent the next four years in the army. At six-foot-four and 235 pounds, "The Big Train" was one of the largest players of his day, with a rare quickness to boot. Upon his discharge from the army, Weinmeister returned to play the 1946 and 1947 seasons for the Huskies as a defensive lineman and fullback before turning pro. Initially drafted by the New York Yankees (yes, there was a Yankees football team in 1948—it was affiliated with the All-American Football Conference), he played two years there before the team and league folded. Picked up by the New York Giants (along with teammate Tom Landry—the same Tom Landry of Dallas Cowboys coaching fame), Weinmeister played four seasons with the team, and despite that relatively short pro career, still became one of three Huskies to be enshrined in the NFL Hall of Fame—a testament to his unique size, speed, talent and impact on the game.

In his post-football career as a key West Coast leader for the Teamsters union, Weinmeister earned another nickname as "The Boss." He served in various capacities during his remarkable 36-year union career, and at one time represented more than 300,000 Teamsters. In 1988, the Justice Department attempted to oust Weinmeister and other union leaders from office amid charges of corruption. The feds were successful in removing some of the leadership, but Weinmeister remained in office and continued his union work until his retirement in 1992 in Seattle.

The King

Apparently Elvis Presley wasn't the only "King" running around in the late 1950s and early 1960s. UW running back Hugh McElhenny earned the nickname while tearing up the grass for the San Francisco 49ers—a career that ultimately earned him a spot in the pro football Hall of Fame. Before that, however, McElhenny was a two-time All-American for the University of Washington football team and set a Pacific Coast League rushing record of 2449 yards in three seasons. McElhenny wowed Huskies fans with a style of running the likes of which they'd never seen before—and perhaps have never seen since. In the 1950 Governor's Trophy (now Apple Cup) game against WSU, won 52–21 by the 18th-ranked Huskies, McElhenny ran for 296 yards, a single-game record that still stands today.

Bizarro World—1950 Governor's Trophy Game

McElhenny played in the same backfield as another Huskies legend, quarterback Don Heinrich. A two-time All-American himself, Heinrich set many UW passing records, and in 1950 and 1952 led the nation in passing. With Heinrich and McElhenny on board, the Huskies offenses in '50 and '52 ate up yards like candy.

With such a stellar team, an interesting convergence of talent and records took place at the 1950 Governor's Trophy. The Huskies dominated the Cougars from beginning to end. Along the way UW thought their All-American QB Heinrich had set a national single-season pass completion record, so they turned their focus to the running game to help McElhenny capture the league's single-season rushing record. Oops! Late in the game, it was discovered that Heinrich had actually only tied the record. Compounding the problem was a dead phone connection to the Huskies bench from the UW booth upstairs. Word about the error couldn't be relayed to the sidelines, so an assistant was dispatched to report to the stadium announcer who announced the record-keeping snafu over the public-address system.

The UW bench got the message, and so did the audience, but the "crisis" wasn't over. The Huskies were on defense with about a minute left in the game, and the team didn't have any timeouts left. There was only one way to get the ball back, and that was to let the Cougars score a touchdown. The Huskies did, then went back to work on the offense with about 50 seconds left in the game. After an incompletion, Heinrich got his record with a short completion to Roland Kirkby. Now it was McElhenny's turn for glory. On the next play, McElhenny took a pitch from Heinrich and went 84 yards for a touchdown, his fifth of the day. The play not only secured the league rushing title that year (itself a new league-record 1104), but it also set a single-game rushing record (296) for the Huskies that still stands today.

How Do You Like Them Apples?

Before UW and WSU played for the Apple Cup, the two teams battled it out for the Governor's Trophy. In 1962, the game was given the current Apple Cup title as a tribute to Washington's famous apple crop.

Storming the Field—Too Soon

Huskies fans can really get into a game, and they did quite literally on October 27, 1962. Tied with the University of Oregon near the end of the game, Ducks QB Bob Berry lofted a bomb from midfield to the end zone where Oregon wide receiver Larry Hill was waiting. Just as both Hill and Huskies defender Kim Stiger went up for the ball, dozens of Huskies fans stormed the field from the end-zone bleacher seats, causing a disruption of the play and the ball to fall incomplete. The referees ruled there was to be no do-over. The play stood, and the game ended in a 21–21 tie. This incident is the reason why a fence stands today between the end zone and the bleachers.

What Size Do You Wear?

In 1968, the University of Washington became the first major college to install Astroturf in their stadium. But because opponents didn't have the proper shoes for the newfangled playing surface, the Huskies had to pony up and outfit visiting football teams with the right footwear. In those days, the Huskies maintained a stock of some 200 pairs of shoes for visiting teams.

Dubious Decades

By the end of the '50s and '60s, the annals of Huskies history were filled with many highs and lows. The "highs" took place on the field, but the "lows" happened off. And what lows they were. After his dismissal in 1955, ex-Huskies coach John Cherberg became a key whistle-blower about a secret slush fund used to pay UW athletes. Though the NCAA did allow boosters to give cash to athletes in the 1950s, the slush-fund payments exceeded the NCAA limit, and the Huskies were assessed a two-year ban from the Rose Bowl.

Enter Jim Owens, who took over for Darrell Royal, coach of the Huskies for all of one year before he left for the University of Texas. It was 1957 and Huskies football was at an all-time low. Two dismal losing seasons came and went before Owens, a tough-nosed, conditioning-minded Paul "Bear" Bryant protege, finally got the Huskies squad to a league championship and, for the first time, a Rose Bowl victory in 1960, not to mention a somewhat self-proclaimed share of the national title with Minnesota. (Long story, but final polls in those days were set at the end of the regular season and didn't incorporate bowl-game results. At halftime of a 2007 Huskies game against USC, UW honored the team of 1960 as co-national champions based on the final results of the little-known and now-defunct Helms Foundation poll that had the Huskies at the top in their final results.) No matter—Huskies football was back, and Owens' place as a coaching legend was cemented.

Perhaps the most difficult Huskies season came in 1969, and not because the team was stumbling through what was eventually a 1–9–1 season. Huskies football under Owens was dogged by accusations and rumors of racial discrimination as early as 1963. During the 1969 season, a group of black athletes on the team requested a meeting with administrators to discuss what they perceived to be unfair treatment. Owens (also the athletic director at the time) responded by requiring every player to give him a personal oath promising 100 percent commitment to the team. He then suspended four African American athletes from the team for refusing the oath. They were Harvey Blanks, Ralph Bayard, Greg Alex and Lamar Mills.

Owens' action came at a time of heightened racial tension within the team and, on campuses around the country, and it prompted the first and only African American assistant coach, Carver Gayton, to quit. Among Gayton's coaching responsibilities was a duty to foster communication and understanding between black athletes and coaches after years of alleged racial discrimination within the UW athletic department, and particularly the football team. The story was national news, and local protests ensued while the four suspended players threatened to file lawsuits and force their reinstatement to the team. Meanwhile, the other African American players on the team boycotted a UCLA game in Los Angeles, forcing

Owens to use red-shirting underclassmen. The Huskies lost badly, 57–14. To make matters worse, during that trip to Los Angeles, Owens' daughter was assaulted by protesters.

Back in Seattle, Owens met with the four suspended players, and three were allowed back on the team—Bayard, Alex, and Mills. Blanks' suspension was not lifted and he never played again for UW. The issue, however, was far from settled. In 1970, there were more accusations of discrimination, more black players departing the team by suspension or resignation and more investigations. Tensions between players and coaches eased somewhat with the hiring of additional black coaching and department personnel, but not everything was completely solved until Owens' own departure from the team in 1974.

The whole affair came storming back to the front pages in 2003, when a statue of Owens was unveiled during halftime of a game against USC. In the days leading up to that moment, members of the African American community, including some of those involved in the 1969 suspensions and game boycott, wondered out loud whether such a tribute was appropriate. But in a touching speech before 72,000 fans during the presentation, Owens apologized to his former players for "any hurt they may feel." For many, Owens' act of contrition provided the closure they'd been seeking for more than 30 years.

Owens passed away in June 2009 at the age of 82. From 1957 to 1974, his teams went 99–82–6 and were credited with breaking the grip and attention that Midwest powerhouses held on the national college football scene. His notoriously tough, boot-camp-style conditioning drills and hard-nose coaching style eventually became synonymous with what fans describe today as "Husky Football."

The Ballad of Sonny Sixkiller

Racial tensions being what they were in the early 1970s, it didn't hurt that the Huskies started winning again. In fact, many people point to a strong-armed Native American named Sonny Sixkiller as the conduit for long-sought harmony between players, faculty and fans. Coming off three consecutive losing seasons, Sixkiller led his 1970 team to a 6–4 record. By 1971, "The Ballad of Sonny Sixkiller"—a song lacking in political correctness—was one of the most requested songs on Seattle radio stations. That same year, Sixkiller became the second Huskies football player to appear on the cover of *Sports Illustrated* (QB Bob Schloredt was the first, in 1961).

With Jim Owens as coach, quarterback Sixkiller led his team to 22 wins in three years. The only thing holding Sixkiller's teams back from true greatness was a running game. During each of Sixkiller's three seasons, no rusher ran for more than 450 yards.

Sonny on the Big Screen

Sixkiller's '70s fame also went beyond his *Sports Illustrated* cover—he scored a part in the 1974 film *The Longest Yard*, starring Burt Reynolds. The college football star played a prison guard.

Burning Down the House

Originally called Soldier Field, WSU's football venue was renamed Rogers Field in 1902 in honor of former Washington governor John R. Rogers, who died in 1901. Disaster struck in 1970 when Rogers Field was razed by a destructive fire thought to be caused by arson. On the night of April 4, 1970, a strong wind fueled the spectacular fire that destroyed the press box and south grandstand as the aging wood around the field went up in flames. The fire is sometimes called the "Sweeney Fire" because then-head football coach Jim Sweeney commented afterward that the old stadium needed to be replaced anyway.

From the ashes rose Martin Stadium, and the Cougars moved into their new digs in 1972 after two years of playing "home" games at Joe Albi Stadium in Spokane. The new Martin Stadium was named after a Washington governor, Clarence D. Martin, who was also a mayor of Cheney, Washington, and a 1906 graduate from the University of Washington. That's right—the Cougars' Martin Stadium in Pullman is named after a Husky!

Martin Stadium was originally constructed around a 440-meter track. The track was removed in 1979, the field was lowered and 12,000 seats were added to bring the total capacity to just over 35,000. However, a record crowd of 40,306 packed the stadium in 1997 for the Apple Cup.

With the 2005 upgrade of Reser Stadium in Corvallis on the Oregon State University campus, Martin Stadium gained the dubious distinction of being the smallest stadium among Pac-10 schools.

The Dawg Father

After the Huskies' back-to-back losing seasons in 1973 and 1974, a rising coaching star out of a small Midwest school stepped onto campus. Don James had just taken Kent State to its first-ever bowl game, and with the Huskies, the new coach quickly showed why he was on everybody's short list. James' first team went 6–5, and by the end of the 1977 season, the Huskies were 10–2, including a win over the University of Michigan in the Rose Bowl. By the end of James' 18-year run at UW, Huskies teams were 153–57–2, marks that surpassed those of Gil Dobie and Jim Owens to make James the all-time winningest Huskies coach. Along the way to this accomplishment there were 15 bowl-game appearances, six Rose Bowl appearances—four won—and a first-ever (official) national championship for the University of Washington during their perfect (12–0) 1991 season. With James, the University of Washington hit the big time as a program of national prominence. James earned his nickname the "Dawg Father" after appearing in team promotional materials dressed as a 1930s gangster.

Moon Shines

James seemed to have a knack for finding and recruiting talented quarterbacks. The first in a long series of great Huskies QBs coached by James was Warren Moon. Moon's breakout 1977 season saw the Huskies go 10–2 and win the Pac-8 conference title, earning James his first Rose Bowl. In that game, the Huskies upset the favored Michigan team, and Moon was named the game's MVP.

Amazingly, Moon went undrafted by the NFL in 1978, so he took his strong arm to Canada where he led the Edmonton Eskimos to five straight Grey Cup titles. Finally getting a shot at the NFL, Moon signed with the Houston Oilers in 1984 before playing out his long pro football career with the Seattle Seahawks and Kansas City Chiefs.

Following his retirement in 2001, the nine-time Pro Bowler was elected to the NFL Football Hall of Fame in 2006. He was the third Husky to be enshrined there (along with Arnie Weinmeister and Hugh McElhenny), the first African American quarterback to make it into the Hall and one of only two athletes to be inducted into both the NFL Hall of Fame and Canadian Football Hall of Fame (Bud Grant is the other).

The NFL loves the University of Washington for the steady diet of talented quarterbacks coming from its rosters. In addition to Moon, Chris Chandler, a third-round pick in 1988, had 152 NFL starts (second for a Husky to Moon's 203) in 17 pro seasons, led the Atlanta Falcons to a Super Bowl appearance and is the only player in NFL history to throw a touchdown pass for eight different teams.

Mark Brunell was a 1993 fifth-round pick, three-time Pro Bowler, Pro Bowl MVP and in 2006 set a new record for consecutive completions (22) in a game. There's also Steve Pelluer, Damon and Brock Huard, Hugh Millen, Billy Joe Hobert, Marques Tuiasosopo, Cody Pickett, Cary Conklin and Tom Flick—all of whom have NFL starts to their credit. That makes 12 players the Huskies have sent to the NFL as quarterbacks—and that's only in the last 25 years!

The Wave Started Here. Or Did It?

Before becoming a host on the popular TV show *Entertainment Tonight,* Rob Weller was a University of Washington student and cheerleader. In the 1970s, Weller taught fans in the student section at Husky Stadium to do a vertical wave during football games. Returning to the stadium as a celebrity and guest cheerleader for a Stanford game on October 31, 1981 (in which the Huskies beat the Cardinal and John Elway, 42–31), Weller had the students try a horizontal, or sideways, wave. The students complied, but the wave didn't progress beyond their section. After a few more attempts to "catch the wave," adjoining sections got the idea, and around the stadium went the movement. Was this the first time a successful wave encircled a sports stadium? It wasn't, according to the state of California's "Krazy" George Henderson. The man who calls himself "the world's most famous cheerleader" says he taught Oakland A's fans to do a wave during a nationally televised playoff game against the New York Yankees a full two weeks earlier. Krazy George has vehemently disputed Weller's title as "The Father of the Wave" and claims Weller copied his idea after seeing it during that televised playoff game.

Apple Cup Is Reborn

In 1982, the Apple Cup returned to the WSU campus for the first time in 28 years. It was a game that many believe revitalized the cross-state rivalry between UW and WSU. For almost three decades, when the Cougars hosted the Apple Cup, the game was played in Spokane's Joe Albi Stadium before a balanced crowd of Huskies and Cougars fans. Thought of as another road game, the Cougars enjoyed no home-field advantage. But all that changed on November 20, 1982, when the powerhouse Huskies instead came to Pullman as the nation's fifth-ranked team, a 24-point favorite and, with a win against WSU, Rose Bowl bound. Ironically, fueling the Cougars' fan and player resentment toward UW was the outcome of the Apple Cup a year earlier when a Huskies victory in Seattle ruined WSU's hopes for a Rose Bowl appearance. The Cougars wanted to return the favor, but as a team with only two victories that year, an end to an eight-year Apple Cup drought was unlikely.

Nevertheless, the Cougars—wearing all-crimson uniforms for the first time since the 1931 Rose Bowl game—were up to the task and used their newfound home-field advantage to stay with UW and even take the lead in the fourth quarter. The Huskies, however, had a not-so-secret weapon in kicker Chuck Nelson. At the time, Nelson had an NCAA-record 30 consecutive field goals under his able foot, and UW was driving into his range with about four minutes left in the game. The Huskies figured to at least make an easy field goal, steal the game again and get out of Dodge with yet another Apple Cup trophy. Not so fast. To the shock of just about everyone in the stadium, Nelson's 33-yard attempt sailed wide of the right upright, his first miss of the entire season. The Cougars added their own field goal before the final gun—it was an upset of monumental proportions. Down came the goal posts and into the Palouse River they went. Up until that point, the Cougars had never beaten a higher ranked opponent.

Why Stop at One?

WSU's Rueben Mayes set an NCAA single-game rushing record of 357 yards during a game at Oregon in 1984. In doing so, Mayes set a second record for yards rushing in two consecutive games with 573. Mayes' single-game rushing record stood until 1989.

The Ice Bowl

In the 1985 Apple Cup game—aka, the Ice Bowl—in Seattle, it was so cold (a record-low 19°F) that stadium personnel had to flush the toilets every 15 minutes to keep the pipes from freezing. Only 49,000 Huskies and Cougars fans braved the elements that day to watch the Cougars "RPM" offense (QB Mark Rypien, RB Kerry Porter and RB Rueben Mayes) upset the Huskies 21–20 after a failed two-point conversion attempt by UW.

Patience Pays Off

The '85 Apple Cup might well have been the highlight of Mark Rypien's college career. A *Parade* magazine All-American in football out of Spokane's Shadle Park High School, Rypien's spectacular college play didn't produce any bowl games. Nor did Rypien's All-Pac-10 Conference Team credentials raise his stock in the NFL draft any higher than the sixth round where he was taken by the Washington Redskins. Still, Rypien became the first Canadian-born citizen to be drafted by the NFL, and after a few years of fine-tuning under the watchful eye of hall-of-fame coach Joe Gibbs, Rypien's career finally turned supernova. As a starter for the 1991 Redskins, Rypien threw a league-leading 3564 yards and 28 touchdowns, including a six-touchdown game against Atlanta. In the 1992 Super Bowl, Rypien and the Redskins ripped Buffalo for nearly 300 yards and two touch-downs before letting off the gas and coasting to a 37–24 victory. Rypien was the first Canadian-born player to win a Super Bowl MVP award.

As good a quarterback as Rypien was, he was an even better father. In 1997, the two-time Pro Bowler walked away from a $1.8-million contract in Atlanta to be with his family and ailing two-year-old son, Andrew, who was diagnosed with a malignant brain tumor. Andrew died in August 1998.

Rypien didn't attempt a comeback until 2001. He started out with the Seattle Seahawks in the 2002 pre-season but was cut before the regular season began.

Pardon Me While I Belch

Former WSU Cougar Kevin Adams still holds the record for the longest field goal in Apple Cup history at 51 yards. It came in the 1986 cross-state rivalry game won by the Huskies, 44–23, during the Jim Walden era of Cougars football. By the time Coach Walden departed to Iowa State the next year, Adams had more than a record kick to his credit—he also had better manners. It seems Walden required his players to attend his Sunday-night manners—or self-improvement—classes during the season. In one such lesson, Walden instructed his players on how to properly expend an unavoidable burp at a formal dinner table: turn your head slightly and burp quietly out of the side of your mouth. Class dismissed.

The Snow Bowl

The Apple Cup game played in Pullman on November 21, 1992, wasn't quite the nail-biter of 1982, or as cold as 1985, but it was notable for the driving snowstorm that plagued the entire game. During play, Cougars receiver Phillip Bobo caught a 44-yard touchdown pass from quarterback Drew Bledsoe but couldn't stop until he slid into a snowbank in the back of the end zone. The Cougars dominated the Huskies in what became known as the "Snow Bowl," winning 42–23 and securing a trip to the Copper Bowl.

Cat Survives Stadium Collapse

On February 25, 1987, during one of many seating expansion projects over the years, a towering section rising above the north side of Husky Stadium collapsed, taking with it a new cantilever roof and 17,000 never-used bleacher seats. Supporting cables had been removed prematurely, causing 250 tons of steel to twist and fall into a heap in about 12 seconds' time. Miraculously, nobody was injured, and even an ironworker's cat—thought to be the only fatality—emerged from the rubble unharmed. Contractors, in their version of the hurry-up offense, somehow managed to remove the carnage and erect another structure in time for the upcoming football season in the fall.

Boating to Husky Stadium

Want to take your yacht to a Huskies game? No problem. Husky Stadium is one of only a handful that you can approach by boat. You can anchor in Lake Washington, just a stone's throw from shore, and then get to dry land by a tender powered by the Huskies rowing team. Thousands of fans boat to Husky Stadium for every football game.

A Kicking Machine

The honor of leading the pack in Huskies scoring goes to kicker Jeff Jaeger with 358 points. His 80 career field goals (out of 99 attempts from 1983 to 1986) set an NCAA record. A first-team All-American, Jaeger once kicked five field goals against the University of Houston, another Huskies record. He also played 12 years (1987–99) in the NFL, scoring more than 1000 points

Once the Loudest

At one time, Husky Stadium was considered the loudest stadium in the NCAA. During the first night game in Husky Stadium history, a 1992 matchup with the University of Nebraska,

ESPN measured stadium noise at a then-record 130 decibels.

Running with the Pack

With an impressive 4401 yards, Napoleon Kaufman is UW's all-time leading rusher. In 1994, he set a single-season rushing record for the Huskies with 1390 yards and was the only UW running back to have three 1000-yard seasons.

The Pick

A budding interstate rivalry between the University of Washington and the University of Oregon was made official on October 22, 1994, in Eugene. The ninth-ranked Huskies marched into Autzen Stadium looking to make quick work of a 4–3 Ducks team that didn't know what to make of itself after beating USC in L.A. and then losing to the Cougars in Pullman. Going into the game, the Huskies were 5–1 with one of the victories putting an end to the University of Miami's 58 home-game winning streak—a high-profile win over the ultra-elite Hurricanes. Furthermore, Oregon players and fans knew all too well that the Ducks' luck wasn't that great against the powerhouse program from Seattle. The Ducks had only beaten the Huskies three times in 17 prior attempts. At least the Ducks had the Huskies in Oregon that day...

The Ducks hung tough and were down 20–17 to the Huskies midway through the fourth quarter. A good Huskies kickoff and a bumbled return pinned the Ducks on their own two-yard line. All Oregon quarterback Danny O'Neil had to do was lead his Ducks 98 yards down field against a Huskies defense that was among the best in the country, and then score a touchdown to win. No problem. In a drive that should live for the ages, he did just that. The Ducks drove nearly the length of the field and scored on a fullback dive by Dwayne Jones to pull ahead of the Huskies 24–20 with four minutes to play. Today, that monumental drive by the Ducks is all but forgotten because what happened next was even more astounding.

As good as that play was, it left too much time on the clock. For the cool and calm Huskies, four minutes was enough to mount their own drive for the win. During the next two minutes it appeared UW was going do just that. Husky QB Damon Huard deftly led his team down the field in what felt like a slow but sure march to the death for Ducks fans. Here were those blasted Huskies doing it again, knocking at the door with a first and a goal at the Ducks' nine-yard line. The ghosts of past Huskies/Ducks games were circling the stadium, haunting Ducks fans yet again. But on the next play, those ghosts were exorcised.

Dropping back, Huard set up and tossed a short pass into the left flat. His target was Dave Janowski, but Oregon cornerback Kenny Wheaton broke early on Huard's pass, made the interception in full stride and proceeded to gallop 95 yards in the opposite direction for a touchdown that sealed the victory for the Ducks. The Ducks more than won the game—they used their newfound confidence to win their next five games en route to a Pac-10 championship and their first Rose Bowl appearance in 37 years. And on that one play, forever known as "The Pick," Oregon's simmering feud with UW exploded into a full-scale rivalry that many fans put above their own interstate rivalries (with Oregon State and WSU, respectively). Washington continues to lead the Huskies/ Ducks series by a wide margin, but Oregon won six games in a row from 2004 to 2009.

An Abrupt End

It seems, though, with Huskies football, there was no middle ground. Vast stretches of unprecedented success were inevitably followed by some level of program turmoil. Things turned for the worse once again in 1992 when head coach Don James suddenly resigned in protest of what he felt were excessive sanctions against the program. UW athletics had been under investigation for a variety of improprieties, including an allegedly unsanctioned

loan given to Huskies quarterback Billy Joe Hobert
from a booster. Cell-phone fraud and drug
charges also were alleged. Down came the sanctions for what the Pac-10 conference called
a "lack of institutional control." The penalties
included two years on probation, no television
revenue or post-season bowls for two years and
scholarship reductions. James was so appalled at
the NCAA and his university for their part in the
penalty negotiations that he quit his job, stating
he could no longer be associated with a league
that treated its players and teams so unfairly.
Assistant coach Jim Lambright took over head-
coaching duties and held the post for the next six
rather unremarkable years. In fact, the sanctions
and the sudden change in coaching leadership
launched the program into a slow but sure down-
ward spiral that took the team to new lows. Up
until 2008, the Huskies went through coaches
like dirty socks.

In 1999, Huskies athletic director Barbara
Hedges surprised UW fans with the unexpected
hire of University of Colorado head football coach
Rick Neuheisel. The new coach managed to get
a Rose Bowl win out of the team his first season
but then proceeded to knock down a notch a program already on thin ice with the NCAA. Exposed
was a series of lies by Neuheisel to Hedges and the
NCAA over allegations about his participation in

a basketball gambling pool. Neuheisel's actions led to another round of NCAA investigations and, in the end, an extension of UW's NCAA probationary period through 2007 (the university was already on NCAA probation at the time because of recruiting violations in basketball). UW fired Neuheisel in 2003.

In 2005, Tyrone Willingham was called in to coach the team and clean up the program. He did his job in that respect, but he couldn't win on the field. Willingham was gone after four seasons that included a year Huskies fans thought wasn't possible...

The Unthinkable Season

To Huskies football fans, the 2008 season was more than a bad dream, it was a nightmare. The once-lofty program of national prominence sank to an all-time low with nary a win. In this fourth and last year under Willingham, the team went 0–12, including losses in the Apple Cup, to the rival Washington State University Cougars, and an ill-timed game against the California Golden Bears in the chill of December two weeks later.

The Cougars footfall team wasn't playing much better. Under first-year coach Paul Wulff, they mustered only a single win before the Apple Cup, and that win came against a lower division (Championship Subdivision) Portland State team.

The 2008 Apple Cup pitted two of the worst college football teams in the country against each other, with the visiting Huskies a slight favorite. The game was notable for a number of dubious reasons, including the fact that for the first time in Pac-10 history, two teams with 10 losses were playing one other. Surprisingly, though, the game was a thriller. The Huskies looked to be winning in Pullman, leading 10–0 in the third quarter before the Cougars pulled off an unlikely comeback that started with a 57-yard run for a touchdown by Logwone Mitz. Then, with two seconds left in regulation, Cougars kicker Nico Grasu tied the game with a 28-yard field goal. Score: 10-all. The Cougars and Huskies traded field goals in the first overtime. In the second overtime, the Huskies got the ball first, but their drive stalled and kicker Ryan Perkins' field-goal attempt from 37 yards was wide right. The Cougars' ensuing drive wasn't much better, but Grasu's 37-yard field goal was good for the win and the 2008 Apple Cup trophy.

The Huskies' loss to the California Golden Bears—a rare December game played on the heels of the demoralizing Apple Cup defeat—was the 14th consecutive defeat for Washington going back to the 2007 season. The 2008 Washington

Huskies were the only winless (Football Bowl Subdivision) team in America. In a rather odd, if not uncomfortable, twist, Willingham was fired with five games remaining on the schedule, but was allowed to coach those final games, setting him up for a lame-duck status that many fans believed only fueled the losing ways.

With new coach Steve Sarkisian in charge in 2009, the Huskies began the season with their 15th loss in a row, this time to Louisiana State University. Finally, on September 12, 2009, against the Idaho Vandals, the Huskies won a game—their first since beating the California Golden Bears on November 17, 2007.

The Immaculate Deflection

On October 10, 2009, the Washington Huskies were trailing the Arizona Wildcats by 12 points late in the fourth quarter of a game UW desperately needed to win to keep their bowl hopes alive. With less than three minutes left in the game, quarterback Jake Locker found tight end Kavario Middleton in the end zone for a 25-yard touchdown pass. Still ahead by four points, the visiting Wildcats needed only a couple first downs to secure the win. Conventional football wisdom dictated running plays to burn the clock and to force the Huskies to use their remaining timeouts. But on the next play from scrimmage,

Arizona QB Nick Foles attempted a screen pass to receiver Delashaun Dean, who could only get a hand on the ball, which then bounced off his left foot and nearly straight up into the air. Huskies linebacker Mason Foster was in the right spot at the right time, catching the ball and dashing 37 yards for the second Huskies touchdown in only 18 seconds. The Huskies intercepted Foles again during the next Arizona possession and the victory was secured—a miracle at Montlake.

The win evened the Huskies' record to 3–3 and gave hope to fans that a seven-year bowl-game drought might soon come to an end. But no, the Huskies didn't win another game until the Apple Cup, beating the Cougars 30–0. And then, despite a season-ending victory over California, the Huskies finished at just 5–7 and were home for the holidays yet again.

Cougin' It

Nobody is quite sure when or how the term "cougin' it" (an expression of failure—or in sports terms, "choking"—when victory or success seems certain) came into being, but most surely know why. The Washington State University Cougars football team has been bad almost as much as they've been good. And all too often, just when a game appeared to be going well for the Cougars, somehow victory was snatched away by the jaws of defeat.

One story has former WSU football coach Mike Price mounting an attempt to twist the phrase to describe a player who performed well in the face of adversity. It didn't take. These days, "cougin' it" still implies failure on some level and can even be heard in reference to another team or game not involving WSU. For example: "Will those Beavers coug' it against the Trojans even though the Beavers are leading in the fourth quarter?"

At Home on the Road

The Cougars are no strangers to playing home games on the road. Motivated by a limited fan base in a sparsely populated part of the state, and by a remote school location that some opponents find troublesome to reach, the Cougars hosted a yearly non-league game at Seattle's Qwest Field from 2002 to 2009. WSU also hosted the Apple Cup in Spokane from 1956 to 1980 and have even had discussions with UW about moving the Apple Cup to Qwest Field—a six-year deal that might have paid each school up to $10 million. But that idea didn't get far. Aside from the upheaval, the two institutions couldn't agree on how to distribute tickets, and the effort fell incomplete. Hoping to attract larger crowds than they could accommodate at Martin Stadium hosting big-time opponents, the Cougars played two "home games" in Seattle at Husky Stadium, of all places. The first game was in 1972 against USC, the second was against the Ohio State Buckeyes (with eventual two-time Heisman Trophy winner Archie Griffin) and both were losses.

"And That's Another Cougar..."

WSU stadium announcer, professor and Pullman mayor Glenn Johnson always gets a little help from the crowd during Cougars football games. When the home-team Cougars get a first down, Johnson announces over the public address system, "And that's another Cougar..."—at which point the crowd in joins with "first down!"

Former WSU running back Jerome Harrison knew a thing or two about picking up first downs. In two seasons for the Cougars (2004 and 2005), Harrison set a Pac-10 conference record by gaining 100 yards or more for 16 consecutive games. During his senior year, Harrison set an all-time Cougars rushing record at 1900 yards and was named an NCAA consensus All-American. Playing professional football for the Cleveland Browns, Harrison broke Jim Brown's single-game rushing record on December 20, 2009. In a victory over the Kansas City Chiefs, Harrison scrambled for 286 yards, breaking the 52-year-old record by

49 yards. It was the third best single-game rushing performance in NFL history.

Last but not Least...

Renowned sportscaster Keith Jackson is a WSU grad, class of 1954. Jackson called his first football game, between WSU and Stanford, in 1952. After several years in Seattle as a KOMO TV news anchor and sportscaster for UW football and Seattle Rainiers baseball games, Jackson joined ABC Sports. In 1970, he signed on with a sports broadcast that lives on as an institution to this day: *Monday Night Football.* Jackson anchored that sportscast for only one year before Frank Gifford took his seat—ABC's first choice all along.

Jackson moved on to anchor some of ABC's most memorable sports broadcasts during a career that spanned six decades. In particular, Jackson endeared himself to legions of college football fans who loved his folksy style and trademark expressions—from "Whoa, Nellie!" to "Fumm-ble!" to "big uglies." After a few unsuccessful attempts at retiring, Jackson finally made it stick in 2006.

Laughing Matters

Rivalry jokes are traditionally bad, and those that circulate before the Apple Cup between the

Huskies and Cougars are no exception. Here are a few examples from each camp (read at your own risk).

Cougars Jokes about the Huskies

It was reported that the Washington head football coach will be dressing only 20 players for the game against Washington State. The rest of the players will have to get dressed by themselves.

Some Huskies were trying to scare the Cougars football team before the Apple Cup game by throwing crackers through their locker-room windows. But the Cougars lit them and threw them back.

Two Huskies were driving down the street after practice. The driver suddenly noticed his right blinker wasn't working and pulled over. His passenger got out and went behind the car to check the light. "Is it working?" asked the Huskies driver.

"It's working," yelled the Huskies passenger. "Now it's not. Now it's working. Now it's not. Now it's working..."

Huskies Jokes about the Cougars

Q: How do you make a WSU grad leave your house?

A: Pay him for the pizza.

Q: What's the longest 10 years of a Cougars football player's life?

A: His freshman year.

And from the Dawg Father, Don James himself, this gem:

"I've always felt that being a Cougar prepares you for life. You learn not to expect too much."

College Basketball—Takin' it to the Hoop!

Ah, Hec

Beloved Huskies coach Clarence "Hec" Edmundson is remembered for his long, successful run as UW's basketball coach. In 27 seasons (1920–47), Edmundson's teams went 508–204. But look deeper at Edmundson's biography and you'll see that he actually started coaching track and field at UW in 1919 before he ever coached basketball. In fact, Edmundson was a track star in his youth, competing in the both the 1908 and 1912 Olympics (but placing out of the medal competition as a short-distance runner in both Olympiads). A native of Idaho, Edmundson was the first person from his home state to compete in the Olympics.

Edmundson put his track experience to work on the basketball court with an invention he called the Fast Break Offense—an exciting style of play that exists in all levels of hoops today. And as to where his "Hec" nickname came from? As a child, Edmundson often replied to bad news with an "Aw, heck," so his mother gave him the nickname he carried for the rest of his life. Hec Edmundson Pavilion on the UW campus is named in his honor. Most people call it Hec Ed.

How Low Can You Go?

The lowest-scoring national championship basketball game in history was in 1941 when the WSU Cougars played the Wisconsin Badgers for all the marbles. Final score: Wisconsin 39, WSU 34.

My, What a Big Nose You Have

Oregon basketball teams of the 1970s—the era coached by Dick Harter—were taught to stand at midcourt and stare at their opponents during pre-game warm-ups. While half the Ducks shot layups, the other half stood near the mid-stripe, hands folded and straight-faced, watching the visitors go through their motions. Knowing this intimidation tactic awaited his team at Mac Court in Eugene, Huskies coach Marv Harshman instructed his squad to don funny noses and glasses (Groucho Marx–style) as they ran onto the court for their warm-up. The counter-measure prompted many of the Ducks players to break up laughing, deflating any air of intimidation they might have had. Pictures in the sports pages the next day depicted Coach Harshman, sitting victorious in the post-game locker room, wearing a pair of the "funny" glasses.

A Lute, a Cougar and a Husky

Nobody's roots for basketball in the state of Washington run deeper than Harshman's. After graduating from Lake Stevens High School, class of 1942, Harshman became a two-time All-American for Pacific Lutheran University (PLU). At PLU, Harshman married the school's first homecoming queen (his wife of 66 years, Dorothy, who passed away in 2008), then coached the PLU Lutes to 241 victories over 14 seasons. He also won 27 games as PLU's head football coach from 1951 to 1957. Harshman's basketball success eventually took him across the state to Pullman and another 155 wins in 12 years as coach of the Cougars. In 1971, Harshman bounced back to the Puget Sound and took over as coach of his former rival, the UW Huskies. With the Huskies he logged an amazing 246 wins in 14 seasons. A two-time coach of the year and Naismith Memorial Basketball Hall of Fame inductee, Harshman is credited with reviving the basketball program at the University of Washington. On February 22, 1975, he was the last man to best legendary UCLA coach John Wooden, beating Wooden's Bruins easily, 103–81.

Small Man with a Big Game

Former Huskies (2002–05) basketball player Nate Robinson is only five-foot-nine, which is short by NBA standards. The New York Knicks guard, however, has a vertical leap of 43.5 inches and is the only player to win the NBA's Slam Dunk contest three times. In college, Robinson also played football and, in 2002, intercepted a pass in the final minutes of the Apple Cup game against WSU, at the time ranked third in the country. His interception set up a game-tying field goal and a win by the Huskies after three overtimes.

He Got Game

By the end of his senior year at Seattle's Garfield High School, Brandon Roy was one of the top prep players in the country. But before enrolling at UW, he considered going straight to the NBA, ultimately withdrawing his name before the draft and becoming a Husky instead.

First-team All-American Huskies hoopster Roy was the first Huskies basketball player to lead in five statistical categories for a single game. That game was on December 20, 2003, against the University of Houston. Roy scored 19 points, made 12 rebounds, had five assists, two steals and one blocked shot. In 2004, Roy led his team to their first NCAA playoff appearance since 1998, and in 2005 the team did it again— advancing in the tournament all the way to the Sweet Sixteen.

Currently, Huskies fans don't have to look far to follow Roy through his stellar NBA career— he's just down the I-5 playing for the Portland Trailblazers under former Sonics coach Nate McMillan. "B-Roy" was named the NBA's Rookie of the Year for the 2006–07 season.

The Ups and Downs of Cougars B-ball

Some of WSU's best years in basketball were during coach George Raveling's era from 1972 to 1983. The Cougars went 167–136 during this stretch that featured seven winning seasons and two NCAA tournament appearances. WSU's Kelvin

Sampson–coached teams (1988–94) didn't see an NCAA berth until his final season in Pullman. Cougars basketball then went into a 10-year funk before fortunes mercifully changed in 2004. That's when the father-and-son coaching team of Dick and Tony Bennett showed up. Dick coached three years before handing over the head-coaching duties to his son and assistant Tony. Between the two Bennetts, Cougars basketball experienced a resurgence in fan interest, not to mention wins and consecutive NCAA tourney appearances in 2007 and 2008.

Raveling's Biggest Score

Before he embarked on a highly successful career as a college basketball coach, George Raveling was a player—and a good one, an All-American out of Villanova. After finishing up at Villanova, Raveling dabbled with a brief career as a security guard. The gig lasted all of one day, but it was a big day: August 28, 1963, the day of The March on Washington during which Dr. Martin Luther King delivered his historic "I have a dream" speech. Working the stage, Raveling was flanking King as he began his exit from the stage following his landmark speech. On a whim, Raveling asked the leader of the civil rights movement for a copy of the speech, and to Raveling's surprise, King gave away his own copy—complete with handwritten notes and last-minute changes King had made himself. Today, Raveling keeps the speech locked away and routinely turns down million-dollar offers to sell it.

The Little School that Could, and Does

With less than 7000 students, Gonzaga University is a small school compared to its fellow Division 1 basketball schools in Pullman and Seattle, but there's nothing small-time about its basketball program. Since 1997, the Bulldogs have put together an impressive streak of winning seasons and NCAA appearances that are the envy of every college team. Considered among the most elite teams in all of college basketball, Gonzaga is almost unbeatable at home, going 120–9 from 1999 to 2009.

Spokane's First Family of Sports

Before Gonzaga became a perennial post-season tournament team, it was best known as the alma mater of NBA great John Stockton. Shunned by the larger schools because of his relatively small size, Stockton gladly accepted a chance to play basketball for his hometown Bulldogs. In 1984, he became the 16th pick in the NBA draft, and by the time he retired in 2003, he was considered one of pro basketball's greatest players. He still holds NBA records for steals (3265) and assists

(15,806), and was a member of the Olympic "Dream Teams" in 1992 and 1996. In 2009, Stockton entered the pro basketball Hall of Fame.

But John wasn't the first Stockton sports star at Gonzaga. His grandfather, Houston, was a standout football player from 1922 to 1924— once rushing for 310 yards in a win over the University of Montana and, in his senior year, leading Gonzaga to an undefeated season. Houston played pro football as well, from 1925 to 1929.

With the entry of the United States into World War II in 1942, Gonzaga football went on hiatus. Efforts to restart the football program after the war never got off the ground, but in only 40 years of existence, Gonzaga football still managed to put two former players into the NFL Hall of Fame: Ray Flaherty, who played with Houston on the undefeated 1924 team before going on to a long career as a pro player and coach, and halfback Tony "The Gray Ghost of Gonzaga" Canadeo of the Green Bay Packers. Apparently Canadeo "suffered" from a prematurely gray head of hair.

Johnny on the Spot

Led by All-American twins Johnny and Eddie O'Brien, Seattle University basketball rose in prominence during the 1950s. In 1952, Johnny O'Brien—who played center for SU despite standing only five-foot-nine—became the first NCAA college basketball player to score more than 1000 points in a season. After their careers ended at Seattle U, the "Gold Dust Twins" went on to the pros, not to play basketball, but to play pro baseball. Drafted by the Pittsburgh Pirates in 1953, the brothers were one of nine sets of twins to play in the major leagues. Johnny and Eddie played together until 1958. Both were out of the professional baseball world soon afterward. Eddie returned to Seattle University to serve as athletic director for 10 years, but in 1969 returned to pro ball when he was named as bullpen coach for Seattle's new major-league franchise, the Pilots. Johnny served several terms as King County Commissioner in the 1960s, and then, in the late 1970s, became head of security at the Kingdome.

Don't Call Us the Washington Generals

On January 21, 1952, Seattle University handed an extremely rare defeat to one of the most talented teams in the country: the Harlem Globetrotters. In an exhibition game hosted by jazz great Louis Armstrong, the Globetrotters seemed surprised by the talented play of the O'Brien twins, Eddie and Johnny, who wanted no part of the Washington Generals' tradition of losing as the comedic exhibition team.

An All-time Great

Seattle University's Elgin Baylor is not only one of the standout basketball players to come out of the state of Washington, but after a lengthy and successful NBA career, he is also considered by some to be one of the 50 greatest U.S. professional athletes of all time.

After leading the SU Chieftains to a 1958 NCAA championship game against the Adolph Rupp–led Kentucky Wildcats (the Chieftains lost; Baylor played with a broken rib), Baylor was drafted by the Minneapolis Lakers—a team desperate for a savior. Team owner Robert Short was counting on Baylor's acrobatic skills and spectacular shooting to win games and keep the struggling franchise afloat. Baylor did that, and more.

From 1958 to 1971, Baylor led the Lakers to eight NBA finals (but never won a championship), played in 11 NBA All-Star games and was a 10-time all-NBA first-team selection. As a prolific scorer from any point on the court, Baylor's statistics pepper the NBA record book. He once set a record for points in a game (71) as well as another record for most points in a championship finals game (61)—a record that stood for 24 years until it was broken by Michael Jordan.

But Baylor could do more than score. Perhaps the biggest testament to his versatile court skills was the record he set in the 1962–63 season with the Los Angeles Lakers. That was the season Baylor became the first NBA player to land among the top five in the league in four different statistical categories: scoring, rebounding, assists and free-throw percentage.

He's in the Army Now

In 1961, Baylor was drafted into the army and sent to Fort Lewis, Washington, to serve out his military obligation. That season, Baylor joined the Lakers whenever he could muster a weekend pass. Still, he only managed to play in 48 games, effectively cutting his 1961–62 season in half.

Close but no Cigar

In the 1967–68 season, Baylor and the Lakers took the Boston Celtics to six games in the NBA finals before succumbing to the Beantown team. It was the closest Baylor came to a championship. He retired a few games into the 1971 season after a 14-year career in which he averaged 27.4 points per game. Ironically, without Baylor, the Lakers won the NBA Championship that same season. In 1980, Baylor was named to the Naismith Memorial Basketball Hall of Fame. Today he is the vice president of basketball operations for the Los Angeles Clippers, a position he has held since 1986.

An NBA Factory

Baylor isn't the only pro basketball player produced by Seattle University. In fact, for a period during the early 1960s, Seattle U was cranking out NBA players faster than any other university in the country. NBA stars Eddie Miles, John Tresvant, Rod Derline, Clint Richardson and Tom Workman all played hoops for SU.

Despite its past success, Seattle University dropped its NCAA Division 1 men's basketball status in 1980 after years of declining resources and interest. In 2009, however, they re-entered D-1 with former Huskies assistant coach Cameron Dollar leading the new team.

SU on the Big Screen

In 1966, Seattle University handed Texas Western University its only defeat in what was eventually a championship season for the Texas team. As for SU, that win earned the 1966 squad a cameo role in the 2005 Disney movie, *Glory Road*.

United Nations of College Basketball

Seattle University also emerged as a leader in racial integration and diversity throughout the 1960s, earning the program unofficial status as the United Nations of college basketball. In the year 2000, SU retired the Chieftains name out of respect for Native Americans, and the school's team name is now the Redhawks.

College Rowing—Racing with the Crew

UW Crew—Rowing the Distance

Huskies football and basketball teams have enjoyed national prominence, but UW crew has experienced prominence at an international level. With a tradition that goes back to the beginning of the 20th century, the Huskies crew team rocked the 1936 Olympics in Berlin, taking gold medals with shocking victories over the Germans and Italians, much to the ire of Adolf Hitler, who attended the Games.

Twenty-two years later, the university's men's varsity-eight crew team was victorious overseas again when they beat Russia's world champion rowers—the Leningrad Trud Rowing Club—in Moscow. Considered one of the greatest rowing upsets of all time, it was the first-ever victory by a U.S. team of any kind in the Soviet Union, and, in 1958, the win came when Cold War tensions were at their highest.

In more than a century of Huskies rowing, the men have racked up 12 national titles and 15 individual Olympic gold medals, and the women have brought in 11 national titles and two individual Olympic gold medals.

Rowing with Ernst

UW crew coach Bob Ernst is a four-time women's Olympic rowing head coach ('76, '80, '84 and '88). Ernst is also the only coach in the U.S. to lead both men's and women's crew teams to national titles.

That's Some "Fine Water"

One reason for UW's long tradition with rowing has to do with its ideal location on the calm shores between Lake Washington and Lake Union. The Huskies took advantage of what the first rowing teams called "fine water," and in the early 20th century UW had one of the most dominant crew programs on the West Coast. Through the middle part of the century, before big-time college football and professional sports found their way to Seattle, Huskies rowing was considered the premier local sport.

Men's Rowing not a Sport?

Men's crew isn't actually an NCAA-recognized sport—the men compete in the International Rowing Association for their titles—but women's crew is an NCAA-sanctioned sport. So why does the NCAA recognize women's crew, but not men's? Blame it on football, which causes a scholarship gender imbalance with 85 free rides available for men at the Football Bowl Subdivision level. As an NCAA sport, schools can offer women scholarships for crew to help balance the scales.

Chapter Eight

Honorable Mentions

A Checkered History

Washington seems a long way from Daytona, Florida—the epicenter of this country's top racing circuit, NASCAR—but the distance didn't stop Derrike Cope, Kasey Kahne or Greg Biffle. Each has won major Sprint Cup races and are among an elite group of NASCAR drivers. Cope, from Spanaway, won the 1990 Daytona 500 after race leader Dale Earnhardt cut a tire on the last lap. In second place at the time, Cope motored past the racing legend for the win.

Enumclaw's Kahne has yet to notch a Daytona win but has 11 Sprint Cup wins and was named the 2004 NASCAR Rookie of the Year.

Biffle, on the other hand, finished second in the 2005 NASCAR standings and then placed third in 2008. The Vancouver native is so close to a championship he can taste it; he has 14 career Sprint Cup wins.

Among the open-wheel racers from Washington, Spokane's Tom Sneva boasts a 1983 victory in one of the world's most prestigious auto races: the Indianapolis 500. Sneva, a former math teacher and school principal, has won a total of 14 United States Auto Club (USAC) races and two national championships. Sneva's brother, Jerry, also raced in the USAC circuit and was the 1977 Indy Rookie of the Year.

It's all Downhill for These Twins

Two of the world's greatest slalom skiers are from the state of Washington, and they were born four minutes apart. The Mahre twins, Phil and Steve, of Yakima, are the last American male slalom skiers to take home medals in the Winter Olympic Games—Phil won gold in 1984 at Sarajevo, and Steve silver. In the late 1970s and early 1980s, the Mahre twins dominated World Cup competition with 36 victories between them.

Climbing to the Top

Long before the Mahre twins were setting records moving downhill, another set of brothers was making tracks going uphill: Seattle natives Jim and Lou Whittaker. Lou has climbed Mount Rainier more than 250 times, and in 1963, Jim was the first American to summit Mount Everest, the world's tallest peak at 29,028 feet (more than twice as tall as Mount Rainier). Jim's achievement resulted in an introduction to former president John F. Kennedy at the White House, and over time Jim grew to be close with the president's brother, Bobby. Jim even headed up the the state of Washington's campaign for the younger Kennedy's presidential run in 1968. Tragically, Bobby was assassinated during a campaign rally in Los Angeles, and Jim later served as a pallbearer at the funeral.

Beginning his career in the 1970s, Spokane climber John Roskelley also made a name for himself climbing the world's tallest peaks, including the South Asian K2 mountain, which is second only to Mount Everest in height. In 2003, Roskelley and son Jess were the first father/son duo to summit Mount Everest. At age 20, Jess was then the youngest climber to reach the top of the world.

Bundling up Makes Good Business

Born on October 19, 1899, on Orcas Island in Puget Sound, Eddie Bauer fostered a profound love for the outdoors from an early age. As he grew older and began venturing farther and farther into the wilderness of the coast, he noticed that the clothing and equipment available was insufficient for the needs of a serious outdoorsman.

On top of his love for spending time with nature, Bauer was also an avid sportsman, and in 1920 he took that love of sports and opened a sporting goods store in downtown Seattle called Eddie Bauer's Sport Shop. Initially, Bauer specialized in tennis rackets, but the creative businessman soon expanded to include his own line of handmade golf clubs and fishing tackle. Business was steady, but Bauer continued to search out improvements and soon developed and patented the regulation badminton shuttlecock that to this day remains the standard for the sport. Bauer's greatest development, however, occurred in the winter of 1923 after he returned from a fishing trip during which he developed hypothermia and nearly died.

"I was climbing a very steep hill when I started to get sleepy," Bauer recalled in a 1981 interview with the *New York Times*. "I reached to touch my back and it was ice. I realized I was freezing to death."

Luckily he made it back to Seattle, and soon afterward began to think of alternatives to the heavy wool clothing that was worn by sportsmen at the time. Bauer knew there had to be something better, and he remembered the stories his uncles had told him about the Russo-Japanese

War of 1904–05. The Russian army was adept at surviving in extreme weather and had used goose-down-filled clothing to keep warm and dry. Bauer bought $25 worth of down and began to experiment with different designs suited to the sporting community. Down is a perfect insulator and is incredibly light, but it can be bulky for use in the outdoor sport market so Bauer added quilting, making the design more streamlined. After several years of testing, he finally released his new jacket in 1936. It immediately became part of the standard gear for all outdoor athletes. In fact, Jim Whittaker of Seattle wore one of Bauer's down-lined jackets when he became the first American to climb Mount Everest in 1963.

During World War II Bauer switched to making clothing and gear for the military and by that time had solidified his name as the top outdoor sporting-gear authority. At the end of the war, Bauer decided he could reach more customers through a mail-order catalog, so he closed down his retail store in Seattle. From 1945 to 1971, Bauer exposed his brand to a worldwide audience and sales were in the millions. The Eddie Bauer brand was synonymous with quality, durability and style, which prompted General Mills to buy the brand from Bauer in 1971. Over the years Eddie Bauer has expanded greatly, with some 500 stores nationwide and dozens of licensing agreements in which the Eddie Bauer brand has been applied to furniture, sunglasses, baby clothing and even an Eddie Bauer edition Ford Bronco.

After selling off his company Bauer continued to venture into the Washington wilderness that he loved. He died in 1986 at the age of 86.

Swimming for Gold

On August 8, 1932, swimmer Helene Madison of Seattle traveled south to the Los Angeles Summer Olympics and won a gold medal in the women's 100-meter freestyle race. Her time of 1:06.8 seconds missed the world record by only 0.2 seconds. Four days later, Madison won her second gold medal, in the 400-meter relay race, with partners Josephine McKim, Helen Johns and Eleanor Saville. On August 13, Madison won her third gold medal of the Los Angeles Olympic Games in the women's 400-meter individual freestyle race in a time of 5:28.5 seconds, beating the world record by 2.5 seconds.

Heavy Medals

Short-track speed skater Apolo Anton Ohno of Federal Way is easily the state of Washington's most beloved Winter Olympic athlete. And after the 2010 Winter Olympic Games in Vancouver, BC, Canada (where he trained as a young skater), Ohno became the most decorated U.S. Winter

Olympic athlete of all time. Entering the Games with his five medals from two prior Olympic Games (2002 and 2006) and his trademark bandana and soul patch, Ohno needed only two medals to surpass former long-track speed skater Bonnie Blair to become the most medaled U.S. Winter Olympian. In his first event, the 1500-meter race, Ohno captured the silver medal in a wild finish that saw him go from fourth place to second after a late race crash between two South Korean racers. Later in the Games, Ohno skated to third place in the 1000-meter event, good enough for a bronze medal and a record-breaking seventh Olympic medal. Ohno was disqualified, however, from the 500-meter event, after finishing second, when a judge ruled that Ohno pushed another skater off the track. In the 5000-meter team relay, though, the U.S. team took the bronze, earning Ohno his eighth Olympic medal. Ohno's 2010 Olympic speed skating team was sponsored by the Comedy Central TV show *The Colbert Report*.

In February 2007, Ohno used his feet in a different way as one of the celebrities on ABC's *Dancing with the Stars*. Partnered with Julianne Hough, the pair won the competition.

Another speed skater from Federal Way figured prominently in the 2010 Winter Olympic Games as well. Remember that crash that vaulted Ohno to the medal stand? That sudden turn of events also moved Ohno's fellow Washingtonian, JR. Celski, to third place. Celski's bronze-medal performance was especially poignant considering his comeback from a serious skating accident just five months before the Games (Celski cut his thigh to the bone with the blade of his own skate and nearly bled to death). Celski was also a member of the bronze-medal-winning U.S. relay team.

Skate City, Here We Come

If you wanted to make the 2010 Olympic figure skating team, you needed to go to Spokane, Washington, to do it. Starting on January 14, 2010, for 10 days Spokane hosted the U.S. Figure Skating Championships. It was the second time in four years that the eastern Washington city welcomed the championship competition (from which the Olympic team is set), earning the town a nickname befitting it: "Skate City, U.S.A."

Never Give up Hope

Even before she stepped onto the soccer field at the University of Washington, Hope Solo had made a name for herself by leading her Richland High School team to a state soccer championship. A *Parade* magazine High School All-American (twice!) by the time she hit the UW campus in 1999, Solo made the All-Pac-10 four times as a goalkeeper while becoming the team's all-time leader in shutouts, saves and goals-against average. But none of that compared to what she accomplished (and the controversy she stirred up) for herself at the next level.

As a starting member of the Women's National Soccer Team in 2007, Solo was benched by U.S. coach Greg Ryan ahead of a match against Brazil. In her place in goal was Briana Scurry, a veteran whose experience against the Brazilian team would better serve the U.S. team—or so Ryan thought. The U.S. team lost, 4–0. The move by Ryan infuriated Solo, and during an interview after the game, the benched soccer player openly criticized her coach. For players to publicly criticize their team is taboo in the sports world, and Solo, considered one of the best goalkeepers in the world, was subsequently removed from the U.S. team—a decision made not just by the coach but also by the players. With the 2008 Olympic Games on the horizon, could Solo make amends in time to play for a gold medal? Yes, she could. Apologies by Solo led to reconciliation and a spot as starting goalkeeper for the 2008 Olympic Women's soccer team. And what country did the U.S. beat to win the gold medal? Why, Brazil, of course. In 2009, Solo became the first goalkeeper to win the U.S. Soccer Federation's Female Athlete of the Year award.

Seattle's First Ski Bum

Seattle's Roosevelt High School graduate Don Ibsen was an avid sportsman and a great salesman. Although a form of water-skiing had been around since 1922, Ibsen was the first to take the sport to a national audience. In 1928 Ibsen began experimenting with various board designs—everything from wooden boxes to snow skis. All failed until he carved out two boards, about eight inches wide and seven feet long, from cedar wood. Success! Water skis were born. Ibsen spent the rest of the summer of 1928 perfecting his new skis on the waters around Seattle. Ibsen sold his first pair of water skis in 1934 for $19.95, and by 1954 he was featured on the cover of *Life* magazine sporting his water skis while holding a briefcase and wearing a business suit and hat.

Pediatrician Knocks out Jack Dempsey

In 1932, pediatrician Dr. John LeCocq of the Children's Orthopedic Hospital in Seattle knocked out world heavyweight boxing champion Jack Dempsey without so much as laying a glove on the champ.

When Dempsey wasn't in the ring boxing the sense out of his opponents, he was often found doing goodwill work in various communities. One Sunday morning while visiting the Children's Orthopedic Hospital, he joined LeCocq on his rounds as he visited his patients. Dempsey happened to walk in on the good doctor as he was changing the dressing on an open bacterial infection on a child's leg. In the 1930s, hospitals did not have penicillin and other treatments, so doctors used live maggots to eat away the dead flesh to prevent infection. Dempsey took one look at the festering wound and keeled over, out cold.

Tragic Crash

On June 24, 1946, the Washington baseball community mourned the loss of nine members of the Spokane Indians minor-league baseball team who died in a tragic bus accident. At the time, it was the worst disaster in U.S. sports history and one that caught the nation's attention.

En route to a game in Bremerton, the team bus had to drive through the treacherous Snoqualmie Pass along U.S. Route 10, a stretch of road with a long history of accidents. The Washington Motor Coach bus carrying the 16-member team had left Spokane under rainy skies at about 10:00 AM. The bus made a brief stop for lunch, had a few minor repairs completed and then continued its journey with no problems, save for the rain-soaked road conditions. As the bus approached Snoqualmie Pass, a car in the other lane suddenly veered in front of the motor coach. The bus driver swerved to avoid a collision but the car sideswiped the bus, sending it veering off the road down a 500-foot cliff into the ravine below. On its way down, the bus rolled three times, tossing several of the players out the broken windows. When the bus finally came to a rest, it burst into flames. Six members of the team were pronounced dead on-scene, and three others died later in hospital from their injuries. The driver of the car that caused the accident fled the scene and was never found.

Best Minor-league Team Ever?

When it comes to an assemblage of future greats, the Spokane Indians hit the mother lode in 1970. Named the best minor-league team in the second half of the 20th century by Baseball America, the 1970 Spokane Indians won the Pacific Coast League title by 26 games. As a Dodgers farm club, the Indians team that year featured Tom Lasorda as coach and future stars aplenty, including Steve Garvey, Bobby Valentine, Bill Buckner and Charlie Hough.

In 1983, the Spokane Indians were purchased by the Brett brothers—George (of Kansas City Royals and hall-of-fame notoriety), Bobby, Ken and J.B.—and the team is now affiliated with the Texas Rangers.

It's Okay to be Different

At Renton, Washington's Liberty High School, Tim "The Freak" Lincecum started out as baseball's 2003 State Player of the Year. After graduation, he waved off draft attempts by Cleveland and Chicago and opted to play college baseball at the University of Washington where he won the Golden Spikes Award as the NCAA's best baseball player. In 2006, Lincecum became the first Husky drafted in the first round, taken by the San Francisco Giants.

Lincecum was called "The Freak" for his long stride, unorthodox wind-up and unlikely velocity from his slightly undersized pro-athlete body (five-foot-eleven, 172 pounds). Freak or not, Lincecum picked up a title in 2008 that is likely to be his favorite: the NL Cy Young Award winner—and it seems to be sticking. Lincecum was also named the 2009 NL Cy Young Award winner, only the third pitcher in major-league baseball to win the Cy Young Award in his second year (Dwight Gooden and Bret Saberhagen are the other two, both in 1985). Lincecum also made the 2008 All-Star team but had to sit out the game because of the flu. In 2009, he made the team again, as starting pitcher. Illness didn't stop Lincecum this time as he pitched two innings.

Respect Above all Else

When it comes to the state of Washington's most successful baseball players, it's hard not to put Spokane native Ryne Sandberg at the top. Taken by the Philadelphia Phillies in the 1978 amateur draft, Sandberg, along with Larry Bowa, was traded in 1982 to the Chicago Cubs for Ivan DeJesus in what turned out to be one of the most lopsided trades in baseball history. DeJesus played only three years for the Phillies, while Sandberg went on to a hall-of-fame career with the Cubs. Sandberg was a 10-time All-Star with a lifetime .285 batting average and a 1984 NL MVP credit to his name. He was inducted into the Baseball Hall of Fame in 2005 and had his number 23 jersey retired by the Cubs that same year. Sandberg's induction speech at Cooperstown caught many onlookers by surprise. Using the opportunity to lament what he perceived to be a lack of respect for the game, Sandberg chastised (though not by name) current players who spent too much time hitting home runs and mugging for the camera.

Dribbling Out of State

Franklin High School graduates Jason Terry and Aaron Brooks didn't play college basketball in Washington, but both are in the NBA, making their home state proud. After leading his 1997 University of Arizona team to an NCAA championship, Terry has played more than 10 seasons in the NBA, including an appearance in the 2006 finals on the Dallas Mavericks team.

Brooks, on the other hand, led Franklin High School to a state championship his senior year and then became a four-year starter for the Oregon Ducks. Drafted by the Houston Rockets in 2007, Brooks scored a career-high 34 points in a 2009 playoff win against the L.A. Lakers.

After winning two state high school basketball titles, Blaine, Washington's Luke Ridnour also played his college ball in Oregon. He appeared in the NCAA tournament twice, and then returned to Washington where he was drafted in 2003 by the Seattle Supersonics. Ridnour eventually worked his way into the starting lineup before the Sonics traded him to the Milwaukee Bucks just ahead of the Sonics' relocation to Oklahoma City.

The Ted Turner Olympics

After the display of petty global politics getting in the way of the Olympics during the 1980s, media mogul Ted Turner longed for an apolitical alternative that promised goodwill through sporting competition. So he created the Goodwill Games, and the inaugural competition was held in Moscow in 1986. The Games were a financial disaster for Turner, who lost $26 million in the process. Turner, however, was a man with deep pockets, and he was determined to see his Games succeed. And so, the second city to host the Goodwill Games was none other than Seattle. The 1990 Games promised to bring an economic boon to the area as some $180 million was put in place for the event.

Unlike the Olympics, participating nations did not select their best athletes; instead, it was the respective sports federations that had the duty of picking the most qualified athletes. The main action of the Games occurred at the University of Washington's Husky Stadium and the Hec Edmundson Pavilion, and the King County Aquatics Center was constructed for the purpose of the Games.

The city was ready to go—even the Seattle Space Needle was adorned with a large gold medal in celebration of the Games—and on July 20, 1990, former president Ronald Reagan attended the opening ceremony and then-president George H.W. Bush spoke to the gathered crowd via video. But right from the beginning the Games were doomed to fail. Ticket sales for the sporting events were far from steady, and of the 3500 athletes expected to participate, only 2300 actually showed up. Turner personally lost $44 million because of the Games, and the city had to absorb some of the lost revenues as well.

The failure of the Goodwill Games in Seattle should have been a clue to organizers to fold the event, but two more cities played host in 1994 and 1998 before Turner finally sold the Games to an Australian company.

Bowling for Dollars

Tacoma's Earl Anthony was the Pro Bowling Association's first Million Dollar Man. In 1975, Anthony was the first bowler to earn six figures in a single year. He won 41 titles, including 10 major professional bowling titles, and was a six-time PBA Player of the Year. *Sports Illustrated* once called him the second greatest athlete from the state of Washington (after Spokane's John Stockton, of Gonzaga University and Utah Jazz basketball fame). Anthony's landmark million-dollar PBA earnings came in 1982, and in 2001 the famous bowler died after an accidental fall down a stairway.

If the Shoe Fits...

In the formidable early days of the NFL, Spokane's Ray Flaherty was a big player, and not just in the athletic sense. A member of the legendary University of Gonzaga Giants football teams of the early 1920s, Flaherty lost just four games in three years. By 1934, he was playing pro football with the New York Giants, and in a game against the Chicago Bears that was being played on frozen turf, Flaherty suggested that his team wear tennis shoes—to better grip the icy surface—but not until the second half so that the Bears wouldn't have a chance to make the same switch. Trailing 10–3 at the half, Flaherty's Giants scored four second-half touchdowns to win 30–13.

Later coaching, Flaherty was credited with inventing the screen pass, coached some of the greatest names in the game, including Sammy Baugh, and put many former Gonzaga players on his NFL teams. As a coach, Flaherty was a two-time NFL champion and was inducted into the NFL Hall of Fame in 1976.

City of Kent Thinks Big

For years, the city of Kent, Washington, went about its business annually hosting two major professional events: the NHRA races at Pacific Raceways (formerly the Seattle International Raceway, or SIR), and from 1982 to 1999, an LPGA event at the Meridian Valley Country Club that often featured local favorite JoAnne Carner of Kirkland. In fact, the Kent Safeco Classic provided Carner with the last of her many (43) LPGA victories. Carner also won two U.S. Women's Open titles during her career. In 1999, Safeco Insurance pulled its longtime sponsorship of the golf event and redirected its promotional dollars to another local sporting venue that opened the same year— the new Mariners stadium, Safeco Field.

Couples is One of a Kind

Washington's most successful modern-day professional male golfer is Fred Couples. Among his 43 professional wins are 15 PGA tour wins and a win at the Masters in 1992.

Thanks, But No Thanks

Puyallup's Ryan Moore might just be the next great golfer from Washington after winning his first PGA tournament in 2009. After a spectacular college (University of Nevada, Las Vegas) and amateur career, Moore turned pro in 2005. He refuses sponsorships, he says, to keep his game pure.

There's a New Game in Town

Even though the Kent Safeco Classic was history as of 1999, the city of Kent didn't lose its savvy for attracting professional sports. In fact, it went to work building a modern new arena smack dab in the middle of downtown, and then found an anchor tenant that raised eyebrows up and down the coast (okay, maybe just in the state of Washington): the Seattle Thunderbirds hockey team, which began play in Kent's ShoWare Center in 2008. Since 1977 (then the Breakers), the

T-Birds had been playing in arenas ill-suited for hockey, such as the Mercer Arena and Key Arena. Still, the team enjoyed a strong fan base and iced some talented rosters, including a franchise-best 1989–90 team that skated to a 52–17–3 record. On that landmark team was Rookie of the Year Petr Nedved who went on to play 15 years in the NHL. With future stars of the NHL playing in Kent, the city couldn't be happier.

Attaway, Frosty!

Last but far from least in Washington sports history is Forrest "Frosty" Westering, the longtime, highly successful football coach of Tacoma's Pacific Lutheran University's Lutes. At PLU, Westering notched 32 consecutive winning seasons, eight NAIA title game appearances and four national championships. Westering's more than 300 career victories put him in the all-time top 10 for wins by college coaches. He's in pretty good company in a group that contains such names as Paul "Bear" Bryant, Joe Paterno and Amos Alonzo Stagg.

Of course, winning games and championships is great, but to Westering it wasn't the most important thing. To him, it was the journey that was worthwhile, as well as the character it took to get to a particular destination in life.

As a player for Frosty Westering at PLU, you learned more than how to run a route, catch a pass or run out of bounds before the clock timed out. You were taught how to run your life, how to be a good person, how to give back and what it took to be successful beyond the field. You developed class and an understanding of the importance of doing your best in every facet of your life.

Westering used football to demonstrate to players how a good work ethic, sportsmanship and a high moral character could pay off not just in games but also in the bigger picture of life.

Players under Westering didn't trash-talk. His teams were gracious to opponents, and stopped play, at their coach's request, to watch a sundown or take a peek at the spectacular Mount Rainier. Westering's signature "Attaway!" followed any number of accomplishments, small or large. His team was even known to shout a few "Attaways!" at bus drivers and fry cooks.

At the end of PLU games, the Lutes never went straight to the showers. Home or away, Westering gathered his players—along with coaches, parents, fans, even cheerleaders—for a post-game ritual he called "afterglow," which was a few moments shared to talk about the game, tell a story, offer congratulations or support, acknowledge a birthday or enjoy the moment in the journey.

To Westering, it was in that journey—through a game or through life—that joy was found. With joy, the outcome didn't really matter because you had already won.

Notes on Sources

Book Sources

Arnold, Kirby. *Tales from the Seattle Mariners Dugout*. Champaign, Illinois: Sports Publishing, L.L.C., 2007.

Bouton, Jim. *Ball Four*. 20th Anniversary Edition. New York City, New York: Wiley, 1990.

Daves, Jim and W, Thomas Porter. *The Glory of Washington: The People and Events That Shaped the Husky Athletic Tradition*. Sports Publishing, Inc., 2001.

Daves, Jim and W. Thomas Porter. *Husky Stadium, Great Games and Golden Moments*. Parker Hood Press, Inc., 2004.

Fry, Dick. *Crimson and the Gray, 100 Years with the WSU Cougars*. Pullman, Washington: Washington State University Press, 1989.

Hogan, Kenneth. *The 1969 Seattle Pilots*. Jefferson, North Carolina: McFarland & Company, Inc., 2006.

Raible, Steve and Mike Sando. *Tales from the Seahawks Sideline*. Champaign, Illinois: Sports Publishing, LLC, 2007.

Rockne, Dick. *Bow Down to Washington*. Strode Publishers, 1975.

Rudman, Steve and Karen Chaves. *100 Years of Husky Football*. Professional Sports Publications, 1990.

University of Washington Huskies 2009 Football Guide & Record Book. UW Athletic Department, 2009.

Walden, Jim and Dave Boling. *Jim Walden's Tales from the Washington State Cougars Sideline*. Champaign, Illinois: Sports Publishing, LLC, 2004.

Print Sources

Ellensburg Daily Record; Kitsap Sun; Los Angeles Times; The New York Times; The Seattle Post-Intelligencer; The Seattle Times; The Spokesman-Review; The Washington Post; Tri-City Herald; Spartanburg Herald-Journal; Sporting News; Sports Illustrated; USA Today.

Web Sources

abrahydroplanes.com; CBSSports.com; collegefootball.org; ESPN.com; fhcrc.org; gohuskies.com; gold-cup.com; goseattleu.com; gozags.com; historylink.org; krazygeorge.com; mlb.com; mls.net; nba.com; plu.edu; reuters.com; rosebowlhistory.org; seahawks.com; seafair.com; http://sportsillustrated.cnn.com/vault/; soundersfc.com; uwnews.org; wnba.com/storm; wsucougars.cstv.com.

Additional Sources

Documentary film. *The Seattle Pilots—Short Flight into History.* 2009.

The Hydroplane & Raceboat Museum, 5917 South 196th Street, Kent, Washington, 98032.

University of Washington Libraries. Center for the Study of the Pacific Northwest.

Greg Oberst

Born and raised on the southern Oregon coast, Greg Oberst moved on to Eugene, Oregon, at the first opportunity. It was at the University of Oregon, that he discovered a love for writing. Now living in Covington, Washington, Greg has turned that passion into a living, writing and producing for radio, TV, print and the web, and along the way writing long-form stories and articles for a wide variety of local, regional and national publications. Greg's love of sports, however, has been a constant, especially his guilty pleasure of college football. From the day this tuba player in the U of O marching band stepped onto the turf at Autzen Stadium, he's been hooked. The pageantry, the crowds, the big plays, the fall chill and a soft spot for amateur athletics—he can't get enough of it, sometimes to the chagrin of his wife of 20 years and 10-year-old daughter.

J. Alexander Poulton

J. Alexander Poulton is a writer, photographer and genuine sports enthusiast. He's even willing to admit he has "called in sick" during the broadcasts of major sports events so that he can get in as much viewing as possible.

He has earned his BA in English literature and his graduate diploma in journalism, and has over 15 sports books to his credit, including books on hockey, soccer, golf and the Olympics.